Human Resource Management in the Hotel Industry

To what extent have hotels adopted new, more sophisticated approaches to HRM? What factors have encouraged the adoption of these new approaches? How has HRM impacted on organisational performance in the hotel industry?

Over the last decade, human resource management has come to be viewed as the dominant paradigm within which analyses of the world of work have been located. This volume examines the nature and assesses the impact of HRM within a highly under-researched part of the service sector, namely the UK hotel industry.

Common perceptions of management practices in the hotel industry typically include work intensification, high labour turnover, lack of training and poor career prospects, and casualised terms and conditions of employment. Using data from a survey of over 200 hotels, this book challenges such stereotypes by demonstrating that this part of the service sector is just as likely to have experimented with new approaches to HRM as is manufacturing industry. It suggests that primary influences on managerial decision-making in the hotel industry are no different from the primary influences affecting decision-making elsewhere, countering the argument that mainstream management theories are inapplicable within hotels industry. Furthermore, where hotels emphasise the importance of service quality enhancement and where they introduce HRM as an integrated, mutually supporting package of practices, a strong relationship between HRM and organisational performance is identified.

Human Resource Management in the Hotel Industry is essential reading not only for students and researchers with a specific interest in the hotel and catering industry, but also for researchers with a wider interest in the nature and impact of HRM.

Kim Hoque is Lecturer in HRM at Cardiff Business School. He has published widely in the field of human resource management, having conducted research on greenfield site establishments, foreign-owned establishments, the nature and impact of the personnel function and ethnic minorities in employment, as well as conducting research into the hotel industry. He is also the co-ordinator of Cardiff Business School's Equality and Diversity Research Unit.

Routledge Studies in Employment Relations

Series editors: Rick Delbridge and Edmund Heery
Cardiff Business School

Aspects of the employment relationship are central to numerous courses at both undergraduate and postgraduate level.

Drawing on insights from industrial relations, human resource management and industrial sociology, this series provides an alternative source of research-based materials and texts, reviewing key developments in employment research.

Books published in this series are works of high academic merit, drawn from a wide range of academic studies in the social sciences.

Rethinking Industrial Relations
Mobilisation, collectivism and long waves
John Kelly

Social Partnership at Work
Workplace relations in post-unification Germany
Carola M. Frege

Employee Relations in the Public Services
Themes and issues
Edited by Susan Corby and Geoff White

The Insecure Workforce
Edited by Edmund Heery and John Salmon

Public Service Employment Relations in Europe
Transformation, modernization or inertia?
Edited by Stephen Bach, Lorenzo Bordogna, Guiseppe Della Rocca and David Winchester

Human Resource Management in the Hotel Industry
Strategy, innovation and performance
Kim Hoque

Human Resource Management in the Hotel Industry

Strategy, innovation and performance

Kim Hoque

London and New York

First published 2000
by Routledge
11 New Fetter Lane, London EC4P 4EE

Simultaneously published in the USA and Canada
by Routledge
29 West 35th Street, New York, NY 10001

Routledge is an imprint of the Taylor & Francis Group

© 2000 Kim Hoque

Typeset in Perpetua by
HWA Text and Data Management, Tunbridge Wells
Printed and bound in Great Britain by
MPG Books Ltd, Bodmin

British Library Cataloguing in Publication Data
A catalogue record for this book is available
from the British Library

Library of Congress Cataloging-in-Publication Data
Hoque, Kim, 1970–
    Human resource management in the hotel industry : strategy,
    innovation and performance / Kim Hoque.
        p.   cm.   – (Routledge studies in employment relations)
    Includes bibliographical references (p.).
    1. Hotels–Personnel management.   I. Title.   II. Series.
    TX911.3.P4H67   1999   99-26139
    647.94 068 3–dc21   CIP

ISBN 0-415-20809-2

To my parents

Contents

Tables

x   *List of tables*

Acknowledgements

I would like to extend special thanks to all those who have offered assistance and advice at various stages of this project, in particular Donna Brown, Steve Dunn, David Guest, Rosemary Lucas, John McGurk, Steve McIntosh, Riccardo Peccei, John Purcell, Kate Purcell, Ray Richardson, Keith Whitfield, Marcus Rubin, Steve Wood and Steve Woodland. Thank you also to Louise for your continual support and encouragement. This book is dedicated to my parents, for their unyielding support throughout my education.

I would also like to thank the respondents to the 1995 Survey of Human Resource Management in the Hotel Industry and the 1993 Survey of Human Resource Management in Greenfield Sites. I should like to extend particular thanks to the participants within the interview programme that followed the 1995 Survey.

Finally I would like to thank the Economic and Social Research Council (research grant R00429424160), without whose financial support this project would not have been possible.

Preface

Human Resource Management (HRM) has increasingly come to be utilised as the framework within which unfolding developments in the world of work are interpreted. However, as a theory, HRM has its roots firmly entrenched within a manufacturing paradigm. In addition, the vast majority of the empirical testing of HRM has been conducted within manufacturing organisations. Yet almost 76 per cent of the working population is now employed within services. Unless it can be shown to be relevant within this sector, what future is there for HRM as the 'dominant paradigm' within which unfolding developments within the world of work can be interpreted? The aim of this book is to address this question by evaluating the relevance of mainstream HRM theory within the UK hotel industry.

The book addresses three key issues. The first issue concerns the extent to which hotels have experimented with new approaches to HRM. The second issue concerns the factors that influence HRM decision-making, and whether these factors are any different within the hotel industry than elsewhere. The third issue concerns the relationship between HRM and performance in the hotel industry. These questions are addressed using survey data from 230 hotels, and both quantitative and qualitative methodologies are adopted.

1 Introduction and framework for analysis

By mid-1998, the proportion of the UK employed population working in service sector jobs had grown to 75.7 per cent. The comparable figure in mid-1986 was 68.3 per cent. Over the same period, the proportion of the employed population working within production industries fell from 25.2 per cent to just 18.4 per cent (Office for National Statistics, 1999). These figures clearly demonstrate the size, the growth-rate and the ever-increasing economic importance of the service sector.

The growing importance of the sector is further demonstrated by the enormous power now wielded by service firms worldwide. For example, as noted by Quinn (1992: 17–20), Toys R Us now earns three times the revenue of the world's largest toy manufacturer and they are in a position to be able to dictate the products which reach the marketplace, how they are packaged, designed and transported. Such is the power of McDonalds that the butter and fat markets collapsed when they took the decision to switch to healthier products.

Trade in services is now the fastest growing element of international trade, with 20 per cent of world trade and 30 per cent of US exports now being service based (Mathe and Perras, 1994). Several key forces have encouraged this process. Firstly, cultural homogenisation has led to the development of key similarities in consumer preferences across nations. Secondly, electronic point of sale (EPOS) technology is now capable of capturing the data necessary to engage in sophisticated international marketing practices. Thirdly, the deregulation of world markets has led to a loosening or lifting of restrictions on foreign ownership (Segal-Horn, 1994). Service products are becoming increasingly sophisticated, internationally tradable and capable of generating a tremendous amount of wealth, and service sector globalisation has become a reality.

This globalisation will inevitably provide UK service providers with overseas export opportunities. However, UK service providers will also have to cope with intensified competition from overseas. In retailing, for example, incursions by European food retailers such as Aldi into UK domestic markets have caused concern (Knox and Thompson, 1994). If the UK is to compete effectively within increasingly globalised service markets in the face of such pressure, developing an understanding of the factors that enable service providers to generate and sustain competitive advantage is a must.

A lack of service-based empirical research?

At odds with the growing economic importance of services is the lack of empirical research undertaken within the sector. As far back as 1948, Whyte, in his book 'Human Relations in the Restaurant Industry' stated that human relations had only ever been studied in a manufacturing environment and that more attention should be paid to the ever-increasing service industries. Replace 'human relations' with 'human resource management' and Whyte's statement would be as true as we approach the millennium as it was in 1948. Gabriel (1988: 6), Rajan (1987: 2) and Shamir (1978: 295) all make the point that the services remain ever neglected, with there being a scarcity of systematic fieldwork, when compared with the wealth of research undertaken in manufacturing industries. Lucas and Wood (1993) make similar assertions concerning the hotel and catering sector, stating that although today's position is an improvement on ten years ago, there is still precious little published. What there is tends to be removed from the mainstream and confined to specialist journals such as the 'International Journal of Hospitality Management', which probably remain unheard of amongst mainstream management academic circles. The importance of services and the extent to which that importance has increased, is yet to be reflected within empirical research, despite the fact that it is studies of the service sector that will shed the greatest light on the future employment relationship.

By contrast, the wealth of empirical research conducted within manufacturing has revealed evidence of not inconsiderable change in recent times, with companies – sometimes drawing inspiration from Japanese transplants, or from exemplar American companies such as IBM – having experimented with new communication techniques, teamworking, Total Quality Management and new organisational cultures, for example. Whether the same level of experimentation has occurred within the services remains very much open to question.

HRM theory: rooted in manufacturing?

Not only is there a scarcity of empirical research conducted within the service sector, but also the theoretical concept which Storey (1992: 2–3) notes has been used to 'make sense' of recent developments – Human Resource Management (HRM) – is entrenched within a manufacturing paradigm. For example, Walton's (1985) highly influential paper, which laid out the differences between commitment and control approaches to the management of human resources, focused entirely on factory workers – service sector workers not meriting a mention. Similarly, the tendency for the services to be overlooked in HRM and industrial relations research is now seemingly being replicated within the emerging debate concerning the impact of HRM on performance. However, the sheer size and economic importance of the service sector relative to the numbers employed in manufacturing, in particular the number of people who actually work on production lines themselves[1], calls into question whether it is any longer, indeed, whether it has ever been, valid to treat factories and the production line as the dominant paradigm by which HRM is conceptualised. Indeed, it is becoming increasingly important for the future validity of HRM to demonstrate that HRM theory, developed within a manufacturing sector 'production line' paradigm, is also relevant within the service sectors of the economy. What future is there for HRM as a theory if it is not seen in the services, within which almost 76 per cent of the working population are employed, as a credible approach? By providing a test of the applicability of HRM in a service environment, this is a key focus of this book.

The problematic nature of service sector research

Researchers are faced with a major definitional problem when looking at services, namely what exactly is meant by the term 'service sector'? This question can be answered superficially by arguing that any firm which is included within Standard Industrial Classification categories 6 to 9 is a service sector firm. SIC sector 6 comprises hotels and catering and distribution (both retail and wholesale), 7 comprises transport and distribution, 8 comprises banking, finance, insurance, business services and leasing, and 9 comprises 'other' services. Immediately, the heterogeneous nature of the service sector becomes apparent. This heterogeneity makes generalisations about the services difficult within empirical analyses, unless care is taken to use accurate industry controls and a sample representative of all service sector firms. To complicate matters further, as Quinn (1992) states, a great number of people working for manufacturing companies are in fact performing 'service' related functions, such as personnel, sales and marketing, finance, legal work, secretarial work, cleaning and catering. Indeed, Quinn estimates that as much as 65 to 75 per cent of the activity within 'manufacturing' firms is actually service related. The definition of a service based firm or a service based job, is therefore not as straightforward as it first appears.

However, the heterogeneity of the services does not automatically lead to the conclusion that a sector-by-sector approach to research will be preferable. Armistead (1994: 28) argues, for example, that industry-level analysis will provide too narrow a basis on which to develop generic propositions concerning the 'service sector' as a whole, and it is therefore preferable to focus on jobs across the services with a similar content. However, this approach would be unable to take into account the impact of industry or sector-specific environmental factors such as product and labour markets, on approaches taken to HRM. For example, the specific seasonal nature of demand experienced in hotels and catering is unique to that sector and is not found in banks or insurance. There may be superficial similarities between the job of a hotel receptionist and that of a bank clerk, but different market and environmental contingencies faced by banks and hotels may result in different approaches to HRM being taken. In testing the impact of a range of external contingencies such as product and labour markets on policy choice, a generic 'lumping together' of service firms could easily result in generalisations, oversights of industry-specific contingencies and a loss of analytical clarity. In terms of operationalisation for research purposes, the 'service sector' is best seen as a generic term encompassing a diverse range of heterogeneous constituent parts. As such, it is preferable to analyse individual parts of the sector rather than services as a whole.

Reflecting this approach, the focus within the analysis to be undertaken here will be on one of the service sector's constituent parts, namely the hotel industry. The hotel industry has seen considerable growth in recent years, with the total numbers employed rising from 279,500 in June 1988 to 318,700 in June 1998 (Office for National Statistics, 1998). However, as Lucas (1995: 14) states, there remains a remarkable dearth of information on human resource management issues in the industry, which, she argues, is all the more surprising given the oft-quoted phrase within the industry that 'people are our most important resource'. The analysis within this book therefore aims to help to fill this gap.

Tests of the relevance of mainstream HRM theory within hotels have several important implications where hotel industry research is concerned. As stated by Lucas (1995: 14), a body of literature has developed showing the sector to be somehow 'different', being characterised by *ad hoc* management, a lack of trade unions and high, possibly unavoidable labour turnover. A view commonly expressed among hotel managers according to Mullins (1993: 1), is that these key fundamental organisational differences render inappropriate the general principles of management developed in other industries, as they fail to take into account the unique contingencies facing managers within the hotel industry. Also, the argument that the industry is somehow 'different' is often used to explain why hotel management research tends to be channelled into industry-specific journals and excluded from the mainstream.

However, Mullins (1993: 7–8) believes that the only substantive difference between hotels and manufacturing is that the customer is inextricably involved within the process itself, rather than simply being the recipient of the product at the end of it. While it is true that the hotel service cannot be stockpiled and production smoothed out to cope with demand surges, and that it is more difficult to achieve economies of scale because site selection is determined by consumer demands, these differences are, according to Mullins (1993), merely contextual. Everything else that hotel managers have to do, for example, the planning of objectives, strategy-making, ensuring legal requirements are met, and organising, directing and controlling staff, is common to firms in all other sectors. Therefore, the theoretical understanding of 'management' should not be any different in hotels than in the rest of the economy. Those who argue otherwise, suggests Mullins (1993: 15), are providing an excuse for lack of improvement. Gilbert and Guerrier (1997) support this position, claiming that there is an increasing realisation of the generalisability of hotel management principles, with managers moving both to and from other sectors of the economy. They also highlight the increasing recognition of the importance of general management qualifications as opposed to industry-specific qualifications. Moreover, given that much of the excellence literature focuses on the individual, it may well be more suited to the hotel industry, where collective relationships are at a minimum.

By analysing the role of HRM within the hotel industry, this book is able to test the assertions made by Gilbert and Guerrier (1997) and Mullins (1993). If it is found that HRM theory provides a suitable framework within which to locate analyses of the hotel industry, there will no longer be any justification to either marginalise hotel industry research into specialist industry journals, or to ignore HRM theory within hotel industry empirical analyses.

The human resource management model

As the aim of this book is to assess the relevance of HRM within a hotel industry context, it is necessary at the outset to provide a definition of HRM. The definition used here draws strongly on the models presented by Beer *et al.* (1984), Guest (1987) and Walton (1985). These models typify the prescriptive solutions offered in response to new challenges it is argued that companies have faced since the end of the 1970s and the early 1980s. As stated by Piore and Sabel (1984), the conditions that enabled stable, mass production systems to thrive in the past, no longer exist. For example, global competition has increased, product life-cycles have shortened, product markets have become increasingly differentiated and increasingly turbulent, and consumer tastes have become increasingly sophisticated. In addition, competition from low-wage developing countries now precludes the possibility of competition on price or cost factors (Beaumont, 1993: 24).

As such, it is argued that Western companies have been under increasing pressure to seek a new approach, involving a re-focusing of activities onto the production of hi-tech, high value-added products. Rather than focusing simply on productivity and cost factors alone, companies must now ensure high quality production, a high level of innovation and production flexibility, in order to be able to take advantage of higher value-added new market niches, as and when they emerge. The new approach to HRM that companies would have to adopt in the face of these challenges is encapsulated within the Beer *et al.* (1984), Guest (1987) and Walton (1985) models.

Implicit within these models of HRM is that if organisations are to achieve the requisite levels of innovation, organisational flexibility and product quality to be able to compete in increasingly turbulent product markets, traditional Taylorist ways of managing and working, well suited to production of standardised goods for large and stable markets, will no longer be adequate. It is no longer sufficient to view workers as unthinking automatons following orders laid down by management. Hence, all of the models of HRM stress the need to generate employee commitment to quality, to encourage workers to take responsibility for quality, to develop systems through which employees can contribute to the process of continuous improvement, and to create an environment where workers feel confident to be innovative and creative. The emphasis is increasingly on what Blyton and Turnbull (1992: 4) refer to as 'releasing untapped reserves of human resourcefulness', and getting workers to go 'beyond contract' – going the extra mile for the company. Getting the 'people' side of the organisation right is therefore seen as the key to the achievement of competitive advantage.

A further source of potential competitive advantage is provided by the inimitability of human resource systems. As they must take into account complex issues of power and resistance to change, effective human resource systems are extremely difficult to copy. By comparison, other resources available to the firm, such as technology, marketing, engineering and financial systems, are all replicable (Becker and Gerhart, 1996: 781). If competitive advantage is generated along any one of these dimensions, gains would be short-lived as competitors would be able to copy the systems developed. Being more difficult to mimic, human resource systems are therefore capable of providing sustained competitive advantage.

The centrality of the manner in which human resources are managed in terms of the achievement of competitive advantage has two major implications. Firstly, it becomes essential that HR concerns and HR decision-making become senior management priorities, and not the responsibility of a separate, sub-board level specialist function (Beaumont, 1992: 21, 1993: 1, 17; Storey, 1992: 26–7). This is one element of what Guest (1987) refers to as 'strategic integration'. Guest (1987) states that as human resources are the most variable resource a company possesses, and the most difficult to understand, they are unlikely to lead to competitive advantage unless fully integrated into the strategic planning process. A boardroom focus on marketing, finance or production for example, will fail to take into account the more complex issues of values, power and company culture. As such, HRM has a rightful place alongside other core management roles at boardroom level.

Secondly, the centrality of human resources to the achievement of competitive advantage results in a philosophy that the precursor of high performance will be the achievement of a set of HR outcomes or goals. HR policies and practices within the organisation should be geared towards the achievement of these goals. The models presented by Beer *et al.* (1984), Guest (1987) and Walton (1985) all make this point. For example, Walton (1985) states that central to the HRM philosophy should be the belief that employee commitment will lead to enhanced performance. The importance of eliciting workforce commitment is also one of the HR outcomes stressed within the model presented by Beer at al (1984). This model also stresses the importance of competence (in terms of attracting, keeping and developing people with requisite skills and knowledge), congruence (the minimisation of conflict between interest groups) and cost effectiveness (both for the organisation, the individual and society as a whole). The HR goals within the Guest (1987) model are – once again – high commitment, functional and organisational flexibility, high quality (in terms of recruiting and retaining skilled and motivated employees, public image and job performance), and finally, strategic integration (the high profile accorded to HR issues within the business strategy and the incorporation of an HRM perspective within line management decision-making). This latter issue is also stressed by Storey (1992: 27), who states that line management should recognise the importance of HRM and engage in behaviour and decision-making which reflects this. HRM should be the intimate concern of line managers. They should 'own', implement and act in accordance with HRM principles.

The HR outcomes are therefore seen as the primary or first order goals of the organisation, which, if achieved, will lead to a considerable organisational payoff. Looking first at the goal of commitment, Guest (1987) argues that committed employees will be more satisfied, more productive and more adaptable, more willing to accept organisational goals and values, and to exert 'extra-role' effort on behalf of the organisation. Committed workers are also more likely to make effective contributions within continuous improvement processes. Moreover, self-directing workers need less supervision, so cutting overheads in terms of managerial headcount becomes a possibility. Also, if the organisation achieves a coincidence of interest between workers and managers, organisational change is less likely to be viewed with suspicion (Beer *et al.*, 1985: 37–8). If the flexibility goal stressed by Guest (1987) is achieved, with a multi-skilled workforce able and willing to move between tasks as the work demands, a more effective utilisation of labour will result. Finally, the goals of quality (Guest, 1987) and competence (Beer *et al.*, 1985) will equip a firm with the skills and resources necessary if the firm is to deal with change in the face of unstable environments.

Achieving human resource outcomes

While the achievement of a set of HR outcomes is seen as the precursor to higher performance within models of HRM, in order to achieve these HR outcomes, organisations have at their disposal a range of HR practices, relating to recruitment, job design, pay systems, communication and training. Particularly emphasised within the HRM literature is the importance of the principle of reciprocity within the design of these HR practices. If workers are to be expected to be committed to company goals, to be flexible, and to contribute towards continuous improvement processes, the company must provide in return fair treatment, a commitment to employment security and to career development, and a removal of status differences between workers and managers, for example. This is an essential principle. Workers cannot be expected to be committed to the organisation, and play a part in business improvement, unless the organisation is prepared to make a commitment back.

This point is argued by Walton (1985), who stresses the importance of practices emphasising mutuality. He highlights the importance of horizontal and vertical job integration, which enables workers to have responsibility and influence over their work. He also highlights the importance of single status and employment security coupled to retraining where old jobs are eliminated and new ones created, and compensation based on equity gain sharing, stock ownership and profit sharing. Beer *et al.* (1984) state that the key HR policy areas of importance are those relating to employee influence, human resource flows (recruitment, dismissals, promotion decisions, appraisal, training and development), outflows from the organisation, reward systems and work patterns. Guest (1987) emphasises the importance of careful selection, job design, the management of culture, and the importance of the development of values emphasising the organisation–employee linkage. As such, both the formal and psychological contracts offered to shopfloor workers should be akin to those typically offered to managers (Guest, 1989: 43).

HRM – its relevance to the hotel industry?

Turning to the hotel industry, the main issue of consideration is whether or not the philosophy or principles underlying the models of HRM discussed here, and the practices stressed within those models, are of relevance. In other words, are there performance gains to be made by adopting the philosophy that as human resources are the key strategic lever within the organisation, competitive advantage is dependent upon the achievement of certain HR goals? In turn, is the achievement of these HR goals dependent upon the adoption of a coherent, strategically integrated package of innovative HRM practices? These are among the central questions that will test the validity of HRM as a concept within the industry.

However, the relevance of HRM within the hotel industry is not simply dependent upon an analysis of the extent to which establishments have adopted the approaches as espoused within the models of HRM discussed above. The mainstream HRM literature contains within it a series of assertions in relation to a range of factors that potentially influence the approach that a company takes to HRM. A test of the relevance of HRM within hotels must also therefore test whether the influences on HRM decision-making debated within the mainstream literature have the anticipated impact within a hotel industry context. The following sections consider the influences as discussed within the mainstream literature.

Factors influencing approaches taken to HRM

Situational contingency approaches to HRM – the impact of product markets

Product markets are seen as particularly influential within the mainstream literature in determining the approach to HRM that companies are likely to adopt. The approach to HRM described above is all very well where a firm is pursuing a strategy producing high value-added goods or services in a knowledge-based industry, for example (Legge (1995: 67) quoting Capelli and McKersie (1987: 443–4)). However, as Legge continues, what of situations where the firm is competing within a labour-intensive, high-volume, low-cost industry generating profits through increasing market share by cost leadership? In such organisations, employees are likely to be seen as a variable cost that needs to be minimised. As such, the approach to HRM described within the models presented above may only be applicable in certain product market environments. In other situations, a 'hard' approach to HRM emphasising a quantitative, calculative management of headcount might be more appropriate. As Boxall and Dowling (1990: 202) state, the full utilisation model of HRM is but one approach to the management of human resources. It is not generic as it excludes all approaches where employees are considered to be expedient, exchangeable factors of production.

This point is made within a range of typologies presented by Miles and Snow (1984), Schuler (1989), Schuler and Jackson (1987) and Tichy, Fombrun and Devanna (1982). Within these 'situational contingency' models of human resource management, the key message is that HRM strategy should support, or fit business strategy. As such, whether or not the approach to HRM described by Beer *et al.* (1984), Guest (1987) and Walton (1985) is appropriate should be contingent upon the business strategy of the organisation, which in turn should be dependent upon the nature of the product market within which the organisation is competing. These approaches are therefore underpinned by what Evans and Lorange (1989) describe as a 'product market logic'. The more successful the organisation is at achieving fit between product market, business strategy and HR strategy, the more successful it will be in terms of achieving organisational outcomes.

The typologies developed by the 'situational contingency' theorists focus on two main issues. These are firstly, product market strategy, and secondly, growth strategy or organisational life-cycles. Turning first to typologies focusing on product market strategy, Schuler (1989) and Schuler and Jackson (1987) base their analysis on strategy models presented by Miller (1986) and Porter (1980, 1985). They state that, dependent upon the product market environment within which a firm is operating, it will adopt either an innovator, quality enhancer or cost reducer product market strategy (Schuler and Jackson, 1987: 208). They must then link HR strategy and business strategy, the rationale being that each strategy will require employees with differing skill levels, differing levels of creativity and concern for quality, differing degrees of willingness to take risks or willingness to accept responsibility and adaptability to change. For example, in an organisation focusing on a cost reduction business strategy, the HR strategy would emphasise the reduction of output cost-per-employee. This would be achieved though the use of non-standard employment, subcontracting and Taylorised working practices such as job prescription, a high degree of specialisation, minimal training and development and a high degree of monitoring. The HR strategy appropriate to firms adopting a quality enhancer business strategy would, by contrast, aim to foster employee commitment to quality and continuous quality improvement. Within the innovator firm, the HR strategy would focus on the development of an environment conducive to the stimulation of creativity. With groups of highly trained specialists working together, the HR strategy would need to elicit a high degree of collaboration, and decentralisation of power to those responsible for innovation. Within the quality enhancer and innovator approaches therefore, there is a far greater scope for the high commitment approach to HRM described above. Where the firm is competing on price, such an approach would be considered inappropriate.

Other models within this tradition also stress the importance of the product market as a determinant of the approach taken to HR strategy. Miles and Snow (1984) look at the rate of innovation as the key contingent variable. The approach to HRM should vary depending upon whether the firm is a prospector (highly innovative), an analyser (moderately innovative) or a defender (rarely innovative). The more innovative the approach to strategy, the more appropriate developmental approaches to HRM become.

An alternative approach is taken by Kochan and Barocci (1985) and Tichy, Fombrun and Devanna (1982), whose situational contingency typologies relate to organisational life-cycle. Kochan and Barocci (1985) argue that as an organisation progresses through start-up, growth, maturity and decline, human resource activities will vary depending upon the stage of the life-cycle reached. For example, concerning recruitment, the emphasis during start-up would be on the recruitment of the most talented candidates. As the organisation progresses through growth stages, recruitment remains important, but attention also has to be paid to succession planning and the management of internal labour markets. As the organisation progresses into maturity and decline stages, managing labour turnover to effect workforce reductions becomes more important. Kochan and Barocci (1985) trace similar patterns within their model with reference to compensation and benefits, training and development and labour relations. Similarly, Tichy, Fombrun and Devanna (1982) focus on the way in which the structures of businesses change as they develop. The appropriate approaches to selection, appraisal, rewards and development will change as the organisation passes through single product, growth by acquisition of unrelated businesses, diversification and multi-national phases.

Product markets are therefore viewed as instrumental within the mainstream HRM literature in determining the approach to HRM that companies are likely to adopt. Within the context of the hotel industry, being a consumer service, it would be sensible to hypothesise that product market signals will also prove to be highly influential. However, it is by no means a foregone conclusion that hotels faced with particular market demands will choose to meet those demands in the manner predicted by the situational contingency models. As argued above, much HRM theorising has taken place within a manufacturing paradigm. There is no particular reason why, therefore, the techniques widely held as appropriate to a quality enhancer business strategy within manufacturing will be deemed appropriate to a service-based quality enhancer strategy. For example, it may not necessarily be the case that the enhancement of commitment is central to the achievement of quality in a service context, and even if it is, the HRM techniques for maximising commitment in hotels may well differ from those used within a manufacturing setting. Therefore, even if hotels emphasise the importance of product markets within their business strategy, it remains to be seen whether the HR strategy adopted to achieve the demands of a given business strategy will be as predicted within the situational contingency models of HRM.

The situational contingency models raise a further important question, namely, the approach to business strategy most likely to lead to competitive success in the hotel industry product market. On this issue, much depends upon emerging consumer trends. Within the mainstream literature, there is considerable debate. Piore and Sabel (1984) in their flexible specialisation thesis, argue that with the saturation of consumer goods markets in home markets, with consumer tastes becoming increasingly sophisticated and with the emergence of low-wage industrial economies in South East Asia and Latin America, Western companies have had to refocus their strategies on the high quality production of specialised or customised goods and services. Similarly, Walton (1985) argues that the conditions enabling control models of management to thrive no longer exist. Product markets are no longer characterised by a stable level of demand for mass-produced standardised products and services. Increasingly, instability, argues Walton, is beginning to affect all organisations. Hence a premium is increasingly attached to responsiveness to customer needs.

However, this argument is not without its critics. Hyman (1991) and Pollert (1991) argue that the extent of product market change is overstated. For example, much of the success of Japanese consumer electronics companies is in mature mass markets reaching saturation, where cost control and the use of mass production techniques is equally as important as a focus on innovation, or the provision of customised or batch produced goods.

A similar inconclusiveness in relation to the nature of the hotel industry product market might also be expected. For example, within the hotel industry product market, it remains to be seen whether the provision of service quality is now more important than price competitiveness or tight cost control. This issue must be addressed before conclusions can be drawn concerning the universal applicability of the Beer *et al.* (1984), Guest (1987) and Walton (1985) models of HRM within the hotel industry.

The strategy-making process

While product markets are viewed as the key determinant of HRM within the situational contingency models discussed above, there is a tacit assumption within the situational contingency typologies that the meshing of business strategy and HR strategy is a straightforward, uncomplicated process. However, several writers argue that this is a somewhat stylised view, which fails to take into account a range of factors that might hinder such a process of integration. As such, product markets may not be as deterministic as immediately assumed.

Firstly, Legge (1995), drawing on the work of Whittington (1993), argues that it is only possible to match HRM policy to business strategy where strategy reflects a 'classical deliberate' approach emerging from a conscious, rational decision-making process. Where strategy is evolutionary or emergent, or where it is processual, emerging in small successive steps, there is no long-term formulated business strategy to which HRM policy can be matched. Therefore, situational contingency models are only able to make predictions concerning the appropriateness of different approaches to HRM in companies which not only consciously attempt to integrate HRM policy and business strategy, but also have a consciously planned, formulated business strategy in the first instance.

The evidence suggests that the classical deliberate approach described by Legge (1995) is far from the norm within the UK. For example, Whipp (1992: 50–1) argues that strategic planning is absent in most British companies. Similarly, Beaumont (1993: 18) comments that many companies in the UK have been pursuing an inconsistent set of activities over the 1980s and into the 1990s, involving downsizing, lay-offs and redundancies, while simultaneously emphasising product or service quality. These activities do not add up to a consistent, coherent strategy. Thus, to use Mintzberg's (1987) terminology, strategy in the UK has tended to reflect ad-hoc formation rather than planned formulation. If the fundamental touchstone of HRM is, as stated by Keenoy (1990), that it is meshed with business strategy, what is HRM meshed with in the majority of companies where such strategic analysis does not take place, or lacks consistency?

Secondly, even where there is a well-formulated business strategy, how likely is it that there will be an integration of HRM with that strategy? It is not necessarily the case that this will happen automatically. Indeed, Mabey and Salaman (1995: 49) describe the chances of such integration occurring as 'extremely rare'. They argue that the process of formulating a strategy, identifying the key behaviours necessary to implement the strategy and introducing the organisational processes required to generate the required behaviours assumes that senior management have been able to scan the environment for key signals, have analysed those signals, and then have been willing and able to reformulate organisational structures. This, they state, is a 'daunting and demanding list of prerequisite steps for any group of senior managers'. This list may be made even more daunting by the fact that, as highlighted by Guest

(1987) and Sisson and Storey (1990), managers within the UK have typically demonstrated a lack of strategic capability and ability to manage change.

Thirdly, the ability to adopt an HRM strategy appropriate to business strategy may also be partly dependent upon the power and influence held by the personnel or HR function. Whipp (1992) states that where personnel management is undeveloped within an industry, the appropriate strategy is unlikely to emerge. This is supported by Guest and Hoque (1994a) who found that where a firm has a well-developed sophisticated personnel department, it is more likely to be pursuing practices associated with an HRM approach, on the principle that it is the personnel department, or the manager with responsibility for personnel who is the most likely to encourage or champion HRM initiatives. Similar arguments are presented by Marginson *et al.* (1993), using data from the 1992 Warwick Company Level Industrial Relations Survey. He suggests that where there is a personnel or HR director at boardroom level there is a higher likelihood of an integration between HRM strategy and business strategy.

However, Beer *et al.* (1985: 27) suggest that a further reason for a poor fit between HRM and business strategy might lie within the HR department itself. If HRM and business strategy decision-making is not integrated, there is the danger that HR departments will develop programmes that line management do not consider relevant. This might occur where there is a difference in perspective between the long-term, people-oriented approach adopted by HR managers and the short-term, profits-oriented approach adopted by line managers. Such differences could explain the introduction of some aspects of HRM in situations where the business strategy suggests a need for a more calculative, cost-conscious approach.

In the context of the hotel industry, the relevant questions therefore concern firstly, whether there is a tendency for strategy-making within the industry to reflect a conscious, planned approach, or an ad-hoc, emergent approach. It is only where a formulated business strategy exists and where a conscious meshing takes place that business strategy would be expected to impact on HR policy choice in the manner predicted by Miles and Snow (1984), Schuler (1989), Schuler and Jackson (1987) and Tichy, Fombrun and Devanna (1982). If strategy-making is conscious and planned, to what extent do hotels make a conscious effort to mesh human resource strategies with business strategy? Also, the ability of management to handle change within the hotel industry, and the relative power and influence of the personnel function may influence the approach taken to HRM within the sector. Answers to these questions will determine whether issues concerning the strategy-making process, viewed as influential within the mainstream literature, should also be deemed important within the hotel industry.

Workforce characteristics

Several arguments are made within the HRM literature relating to the potential impact of workforce characteristics on HRM policy choice. Firstly, Beer *et al.* (1985: 25) raise the contention that the motivation, capacities and potential of the workforce will restrict policy choices available to management. Similarly, Guest (1987) states that many workers will not wish to show high intrinsic motivation at work, and thus attempts to apply innovative HRM techniques to an established workforce will not always be practical (Guest 1987: 516). The adoption of HRM will therefore be restricted if the workforce proves resistant to change, or where working practices are entrenched. The take up of HRM may be proportionately higher on greenfield sites where management are given a clean slate, and where they do not have to fight against existing attitudes and existing systems of industrial relations (Guest and Hoque, 1993).

Relating to workforce skill levels, Beaumont (1993: 26–7) and Keep (1989) argue that the deficiencies in skills training and in vocational education in the UK, as highlighted by Finegold and Soskice (1988), will potentially hamper the introduction of HRM. Supporting this view, Hendry and Pettigrew (1990: 28) refer to research by Daly, Hitchens and Wagner (1985) and Steedman and Wagner (1987) which examines matched pairs of German and British metal-working and kitchen furniture manufacturers. The research demonstrated that the lack of availability of workers with high-level skills in the UK influenced firms' decisions to concentrate production on the cheaper, mass-produced end of the market.

Existing workforce characteristics are therefore seen as a critical determinant of the approach taken to HRM within the mainstream HRM literature. It is likely that workforce characteristics will be viewed as an equally important determinant within the hotel industry. To assess this issue, it will be necessary to evaluate the extent to which the hotel industry workforce is likely to prove amenable, or is likely to respond to HRM. It may be the case, for example, that overall skill and training levels are too low for an HRM approach to prove viable. Similarly, resistance to change may present a problem. These questions will need to be addressed if it is to be ascertained whether the arguments concerning the influence of workforce characteristics on the approach taken to HRM discussed within the mainstream literature are relevant within the hotel industry.

The impact of trade unions

It is commonly argued that a trade union presence will militate against the adoption of HRM. Where a union is present, union officials might resist the introduction of innovative HRM practices. In particular, they are likely to resist practices emphasising direct communication between management and employees, thus bypassing traditional union collective bargaining channels. They are also likely to resist practices attempting to elicit employee commitment to the organisation and hence result in a reduction of the perceived need for a trade union amongst the workforce. HRM practices, Beaumont (1992: 35) claims, with their emphasis on teamwork, flexibility, employee involvement, participation and commitment, 'drive a wedge' between unions and their members and is therefore logical for union officials to resist the introduction of such practices.

Conversely, it has often been argued that a lack of trade unions will facilitate the adoption of HRM. As Beer *et al.* (1985: 32–3) argue, non-union firms will invest heavily in HRM policies including employment security, grievance procedures and open-door policies, maybe offering terms and conditions which are more generous than those in unionised companies, in order to maintain their non-union status.

However, Guest (1995) presents a different viewpoint. He argues that there is a great deal in common between HRM and trade union objectives. For example, both emphasise the achievement of status reductions, job security, skill enhancement and high basic pay. Guest (1995) also argues that much of what has been introduced in the UK under the description of HRM has been piecemeal, unstrategic and somewhat half-hearted, and has had little impact on performance. As such, he argues that unions should champion the introduction of a more strategic HRM approach, instrumentally encouraging management and assisting them in the implementation of high-quality management practices, and also ensuring there is no slippage in the operation of those practices. The union's role therefore becomes one of 'internal consultant', and is legitimated in the eyes of management, as they realise the benefits of joint partnership. This approach is supported by the Trades Union Congress (1994), who argue that unions can play a highly influential role in developing a 'world class workplace'.

The debate within the mainstream HRM literature concerning the relationship between unions and HRM is therefore somewhat inconclusive. In the context of the hotel industry, it will be somewhat difficult to test empirically the impact of trade unions on HRM, given the lack of recognised trade unions within the industry. Nevertheless, it will be possible to develop hypotheses as to whether managers take advantage of the non-union nature of the industry to experiment with new approaches to HRM or to adopt labour-intensifying or cost-cutting practices.

The impact of labour markets

Beer *et al.* (1985: 31–2) argue that where labour market conditions are tight, companies are under increased pressure to ensure the recruitment and retention of the most qualified and capable employees. As such, there will be a greater emphasis on policies relating to wages, career advancement and working conditions likely to attract and keep such staff. Similarly, Ramsay (1991) claims that under tight labour market conditions, managers threatened with potential control loss will attempt to incorporate the workforce by allowing them to participate in management decision-making, thus stifling conflict. As soon as conditions allow, however, they return to a more direct approach. As far as the hotel industry is concerned, this debate raises the question as to whether there is any labour market pressure on management to adopt practices that encourage the recruitment and retention of the most able staff, or to adopt practices aimed at averting workforce recalcitrance.

Organisation characteristics

It is widely acknowledged that in very small establishments, formal HRM practices may be inappropriate. For example, effective communication may be achieved via informal face-to-face contact rather than via expensive and complex formal communication techniques. As such, HRM may be inappropriate within small seaside resort hotels employing only a handful of staff. It will therefore be necessary to take into account establishment size when assessing the extent to which HRM is practised within the hotel industry, or at least the level within the organisation at which it is likely to be practised.

National ownership

A body of literature has developed concerning the relationship between ownership and HRM. Examples include the research on Japanese management (for example Oliver and Wilkinson, 1989, 1992; Trevor and White, 1983; Wickens, 1987; Wood, 1996), which demonstrates that Japanese firms, on the whole, have adopted a more strategic approach to HRM than have their UK-owned counterparts. More recently, attention has focused on establishments from other national origins. For example, Beaumont, Cressey and Jakobsen (1990), Guest (1996) and Guest and Hoque (1996) find a surprising lack of interest in techniques associated with an HRM approach amongst German-owned firms operating within the UK. The impact of national ownership on the approach taken to HRM within the hotel industry is worthy of further consideration, particularly if a relationship between HRM and performance can be identified.

Impact of financial markets

According to Kirkpatrick, Davies and Oliver (1992: 132) and Purcell (1989: 69–71), there has been a rapid trend towards diversification and divisionalisation within the UK. This is because in the UK, the stock market emphasis on short-term financial results has encouraged a policy of decentralisation, as companies attempt to ensure a regular positive cash-flow by operating in a range of product markets, all of which will mature at different times (Sisson and Storey, 1990). This in turn has led to the adoption of M-form company organisation, which is seen as the best way of managing a diversified business. The enterprise is therefore not seen as a unified business but as a collection of businesses.

However, M-form structures render infeasible the concept of a corporate-wide HR strategy. This is because each segment of the business will require different approaches to HRM, depending upon the product market and upon the stage in the product life-cycle reached. HRM decision-making is therefore devolved to divisional level. In the absence of an HRM presence at corporate level however, financial criteria, management accounting, tighter short-run financial controls (Armstrong, 1989) and high accountability of divisional profits (Purcell, 1989) will come to dominate. Such pressure to achieve results in financial terms will preclude the longer term developmental activities relevant to the 'soft' motivation and commitment-oriented aspects of HRM (Kirkpatrick, Davies and Oliver, 1992: 142–3). Even if line management had an interest in pursuing HRM goals or where the product market suggested HRM to be applicable, such approaches would be precluded by the immediate imperative of short-term financial performance targets imposed by the corporate centre (Sisson and Storey, 1990).

According to Storey (1992: 43), the arguments presented above may well be overstated. He states that there is considerable variation between the HR policies adopted by the divisions within M-form companies, which suggests that there are other factors influencing management behaviour other than simply company structure. He questions whether or not it would be possible to develop unit level HR strategies without corporate management support, and also notes that competition for investment funds within a group is often dependent upon the ability to demonstrate that advances have been made in terms of HRM.

Nevertheless, the relevance of this debate to the hotel industry will depend upon whether there is any pressure from decentralisation as described by Armstrong (1989), Kirkpatrick, Davies and Oliver (1992) and Purcell (1989) within the hotel industry. If so, it will also be possible to test the extent to which that pressure is likely to restrict the adoption of an HRM approach.

Summary

This chapter has developed a framework that outlines the models of HRM as presented by Beer *et al.* (1984), Guest (1987) and Walton (1985), and highlights the factors that are likely to encourage or restrict the implementation of the approach to HRM as encapsulated within those models. The framework demonstrates that the likely adoption of HRM is dependent upon a range of influences relating to product markets, the resourcing of the personnel department, the ability of managers to handle change effectively, workforce characteristics, union presence, labour market conditions, organisational size, national ownership and financial markets.

The aim of this book is to test the validity of this framework within a service industry context, namely the hotel industry. The first test of the relevance of HRM in the hotel industry concerns the extent to which practices associated with an HRM approach have been adopted. The second test concerns the factors that are likely to influence the approach taken to HRM, in particular, whether the factors viewed as influential within the mainstream HRM literature are also viewed as important within the hotel industry. If managers within the industry have to contend with a range of contingencies not taken into account within the mainstream debates, the suggestion will be that the hotels are indeed somehow 'different', and that the framework outlined above is of limited relevance.

The final test of the relevance of HRM within the hotel industry concerns the relationship between HRM and performance. This is a critical question concerning the applicability of HRM – it would only prove sensible to encourage the wider adoption of HRM in the industry if it can be demonstrated that HRM has a contribution to make to superior performance.

The book tests these issues in the following manner. The following chapter examines the factors that will potentially influence the approach taken to HRM within the hotel industry, and develops hypotheses relating to the likely impact of these factors. This chapter also develops hypotheses concerning the impact of factors not discussed within the mainstream literature that are considered important within the hotel industry. In drawing out the differences and similarities between the factors seen as potential influences on the approach taken to HRM discussed within the two sets of literature, this is a key chapter in determining the applicability of HRM theory within a hotel industry context.

The subsequent chapters test the hypotheses developed, taking a quantitative empirical approach to examine the extent to which HRM has been adopted, the factors influencing the approach taken to HRM, and also the relationship between HRM and organisational performance. Chapter 3 introduces the empirical underpinning of the book, namely the 1995 Survey of Human Resource Management in the Hotel Industry. Data generated within this survey are compared with data from a sample of manufacturing establishments, to assess from a comparative perspective the extent to which practices associated with an HRM approach have been adopted within the industry. Chapter 4 uses data from the 1995 Survey of Human Resource Management in the Hotel Industry to examine empirically the factors influencing the approach taken to HRM. Chapter 5 provides a corroboration of the results achieved within Chapters 3 and 4 from a qualitative perspective.

Chapter 6 looks at performance issues. A number of studies have recently ascertained a link between HRM and performance. These studies include Arthur (1994), Guest and Hoque (1994b, 1996), Huselid (1995), Ichniowski, Shaw and Prennushi (1994) and MacDuffie (1995). Chapter 6 assesses whether similar performance effects can be identified within the hotel industry. In a similar vein to the multivariate analyses undertaken within earlier studies of the impact of HRM on performance, this chapter evaluates the relationship between HRM and performance within the hotel industry, and also the circumstances within which HRM contributes to superior performance.

Note

1   Littler (1989:19) estimates that in 1982 only about 1.4 million people worked in a mass production industry, and the number of direct workers on the line was only half that number.

2   Is there a role for HRM in the hotel industry?

This chapter has two main aims. The first is to examine existing character-isations of HRM in the hotel industry. The industry has been conventionally characterised as labour intensive and exploitative, with there being little or no scope for developmental approaches to HRM, especially where more junior staff grades are concerned. In addition, hotel industry managers have often been accused of lacking long-term strategic vision.

The second aim of the chapter is to begin to examine the factors that influence decision-making in relation to HRM within the industry. This will not only enable the development of testable hypotheses concerning the factors that are likely to influence the approach taken to HRM within hotels, but it will also enable an analysis of the extent to which the factors commonly seen as important influences on HRM within the mainstream literature are also seen as important by hotel industry researchers. The extent to which there is common ground between the two is an important test of the relevance of mainstream HRM theory within the hotel industry.

Within the hotel industry literature, whether or not the influences discussed suggest a potential role for HRM is by no means a clear-cut issue. There are compelling arguments to suggest that tight cost control is essential if hotels are to remain competitively viable. However, there are also equally compelling arguments that as service quality becomes increasingly important for competi-tive success, so does the need for a committed and motivated workforce, and management will not achieve this commitment if they treat their workers as disposable resources. However, even if service quality is considered important, policy choice may be restricted by a lack of workforce willingness to change, entrenched working patterns and employment instability, for example. These arguments will be looked at in the second part of the chapter.

The first section looks at the research undertaken to date that characterises the management of human resources in the hotel industry.

What characterises HRM in the hotel industry?

Considerable debate has emerged recently concerning the degree of experimentation with new approaches to HRM within the hotel industry. Conventionally,
descriptions of the industry have emphasised an autocratic management style
and a reluctance on the part of managers to allow employees any influence
over work processes or their working environment (Macfarlane, 1982: 39).
Management's primary strategic control has tended to emphasise a tight control
over costs.

This conventional depiction is supported by a number of empirical studies.
For example, Guerrier and Lockwood (1989a: 86–7) found that that where
hotels had experimented with joint consultative committees, project teams,
staff development exercises and employee involvement, such initiatives had
more to do with increasing management control rather than developing a
sense of commitment.

Hales' (1987) survey yielded encouraging results at first glance concerning
the extent to which HRM-type practices had been adopted. Of the 32 establishments within his sample, none had worker directors, only 22 per cent had
autonomous work groups and only 15 per cent used quality circles. However,
job rotation was found in 55 per cent of hotels, job enlargement in 68 per
cent, job enrichment in 59 per cent, project teams in 68 per cent, and works
councils in 43 per cent.

These percentages, Hales (1987: 263) concedes, might have been somewhat
high, in that only those with something to report may have replied to the
questionnaire. More importantly though, a more in-depth analysis revealed a
considerable emphasis on labour intensification and a high degree of managerial
control. As became evident in the 15 follow-up interviews, the manner in
which the respondents interpreted the meaning of the practices asked about
varied greatly. In some establishments, job rotation simply meant management
moving between departments. Job enrichment and enlargement were, on the
whole, used to give extra responsibility to specific staff, often management, or
as a means of rationalising the management structure in order to reduce headcount. Individual development tended to be considered a side-issue. The works
councils found within the survey were often used simply to legitimate
managerial decisions, or to discuss routine matters such as menus or staff
uniforms. Project teams were only in evidence at management level.

The primary intentions behind the introduction of the techniques asked
about within the survey were therefore either to enhance managerial control,
or to improve productivity via job loading. No attempt was made to disguise

this. Indeed Hales (1987: 271) states that there was a readiness on the part of management to admit that techniques were used for these purposes. Also, most initiatives applied exclusively to management, there being a general perception that non-management employees did not want any greater responsibility.

Lockwood and Guerrier (1989) found a similar lack of interest in developmental approaches to HRM in their study of 15 major UK hotel groups. Only one company displayed any evidence of functional flexibility and multi-skilling. Short-term contracts were used to deal with seasonal variation, and part-time working was used to deal with daily or weekly variation. Such practices reflected a managerial desire to run a 'tight ship' – matching headcount to variations in demand as closely as possible. A further study undertaken by Guerrier and Lockwood (1989b) looked more formally at the issue of functional and numerical flexibility with reference to Atkinson's (1984) core-periphery model. They found that management alone fitted the description of 'company' core staff – those who had career prospects, were multi-skilled and were geographically flexible. They found little evidence of the development of internal career paths, with up to 80 per cent of vacancies being filled from the external labour market.

This reliance on numerical flexibility has also been demonstrated within macro-level research looking at emerging employment trends in the industry. Looking at the hospitality industry as a whole, between 1971 and 1981 there was an increase in numbers employed from 680,000 to 922,000, a 36 per cent growth rate which far outstripped that of services as a whole which saw a 15 per cent increase over the same period (Robinson and Wallace, 1984). However, this job growth was due almost entirely to a growth in part-time working. Of the 242,000 jobs created, 192,000 were accounted for by women and 38,000 by men working less than 30 hours a week. Full-time female employment actually fell by 4000, with male full-time jobs increasing by only 18,000. By 1981, part-time working in the industry constituted 57 per cent of male total employment and 67 per cent of total female employment.

This trend continued into the 1980s. Using Department of Employment quarterly estimates and the New Earnings Survey to examine job growth in the hospitality industry, Lucas (1993) found that between 1980 and 1990, employment in the industry grew to 1.256 million. Growth was faster in the latter part of the decade in response to the consumer boom. However, as in the 1970s, the main area of job growth was in part-time employment. What is more, there was a disproportionate growth in part-time workers working less than 16 hours per week. This may partly have been explained by the growth in young workers in the fast food sector and the growing pressure on young people such as students to join the labour market. Nevertheless, the trend towards the increased use of part-time working would seem to indicate management's penchant for numerically flexible labour. Such working patterns enable wage bills to be reduced, as employers can avoid both National Insurance contributions and also the provision of statutory benefits such as maternity leave and sick pay (Lucas, 1993: 25).

However, while many studies undertaken in the past have revealed little interest in HRM in the hotel industry, a growing number of more recent studies are beginning to suggest a different picture. For example, Harrington and Akehurst (1996) found that 87 per cent of hotels within their sample considered quality to be a strategic concern, with 82 per cent having invested resources to train employees in quality-related endeavours. Anastassova and Purcell (1995) found that managers, particularly those in larger hotels, had moved away from a directive and autocratic style, towards a consultative approach. They also found managers to have been trained in Total Quality Management and regarding themselves as practising HRM rather than personnel management.

In a similar vein, Buick and Muthu (1997) found within their survey of hotels in Scotland, that the development of internal labour markets and career development had assumed an increased importance. Watson and D'Annunzio-Green (1996), in their study of two large hotels, found appraisal systems, training and development, communication systems and extensive consultation had been introduced in order to support a culture of service quality. Gilbert and Guerrier (1997: 122) argue that managers have increasingly taken on board notions of empowerment and teamworking and the need to devolve responsibility to lower levels.

However, reflecting the development of considerable debate over the extent to which there has been change within the industry in recent years, not all the recent accounts demonstrate an improvement. For example, Price (1994: 52) argues that there is a worrying lack of basic professionalism in the conduct of personnel management. Within her sample, only 39 per cent referred to all the terms and conditions stipulated in the Employment Protection Consolidation Act (1978), and only 24 per cent referred to all the disciplinary procedures in the Arbitration Conciliation Advisory Service (ACAS) code of practice. Word-of-mouth contact remained the most common source of recruitment for low-skill staff. While Price (1994) concedes that there may have been a degree of improvement among larger hotels, she concludes that there remains a dearth of sophisticated human resource practices within the industry. Indeed, she argues that research on employment-related issues within an HRM framework would be meaningless given that the industry is so far removed from the HRM 'ideal type' (Price 1994: 48).

Similarly, Lucas (1995: 90) maintains that a lack of innovation remains the norm within the industry, and she argues that there is little evidence that any kind of HRM approach is being followed even among larger organisations. Although conceding that the data are not sufficient for a definitive conclusion, she suggests that the industry would fit within the 'bad' or 'ugly' categories of the typology presented by Guest and Hoque (1994b), or the bleak environments described by Sisson (1993). Teare (1996) supports this position, arguing that although some organisations are beginning to experiment with new techniques, the bulk of the evidence suggests that the sector remains bound by traditional working methods and employment practices.

Factors influencing HRM decision-making in the hotel industry

As demonstrated above, the conventional view of the hotel industry is that it remains backward in its approach to HRM. Where innovative management techniques have been experimented with, they have been used primarily to intensify work effort, rather than to enhance commitment.

While there has been some recent debate over the extent to which this conventional picture remains valid, with a few studies presenting anecdotal accounts of experimentation with new HRM techniques, others continue to report the industry as still failing to adopt a more strategic approach. The next section aims to develop hypotheses as to why this might be the case, considering the factors that might influence HRM policy choice within the hotel industry. The following section also assesses the extent to which there is common ground between the influences on HRM considered important in the mainstream HRM literature and the influences considered important within the hotel industry.

Product markets and competitive strategy

The impact of product markets on the approach taken to HRM is emphasised within the situational contingency models presented by Kochan and Barocci (1985), Miles and Snow (1984), Schuler and Jackson (1987) and Tichy, Fombrun and Devanna (1982). These models, discussed within the first chapter, all emphasise the relationship between product markets and business strategy, and the relationship between business strategy and HRM policy choice. The models suggest that where there is scope for diversity in business strategies within any given industry, there is likewise scope for diversity in the approaches taken to HRM.

Are product markets also viewed as an important influence on HRM policy choice within the hotel industry? Perhaps not surprisingly, given the nature of the hotel industry as a consumer service, product market signals are indeed seen to have a considerable impact. Moreover, as is the case within the mainstream HRM literature (see for example, Piore and Sabel, 1984; Hyman, 1991; Pollert, 1991), the precise nature of product markets is subject to debate. A few commentators consider the market to be price-led, while many increasingly consider quality enhancement to be the key to competitive success. The following section looks at these viewpoints in detail.

Price competition

In an examination of consumer trends, Shamir (1978: 302), argues that hotel clientele is increasingly being drawn from a wider social base. A declining proportion of the market is looking for the sort of personalised service offered in the days when the industry catered solely for the higher classes. While service quality remains important, what is now required is adherence to standards guaranteeing a certain level of quality, rather than customised quality tailored to suit the needs of individual customers.

Shamir (1978: 302–3) also argues that technological change, in particular, the introduction of vending machines and technology enabling customer self-service, facilitates increased product automation and a decrease in direct customer–staff contact. This renders the service process more controllable and more easily governable by rules and regulations. Such mechanisation is found in particular, according to Shamir, in budget hotel chains, where standardisation of service is marketed as an assurance of a specified degree of service quality.

This viewpoint is supported by research conducted by Larmour (1983: 91), who found managers to emphasise the importance of cost control more than the importance of quality enhancement. Following in-depth, semi-structured interviews with 42 managers, he found that in response to rising costs and the reduced spending power of customers, hotels had implemented cost-cutting exercises and focused on price issues within their marketing strategies. Of course, this finding may be related to the time the research was undertaken (during the recession of the early 1980s), but it may have had a cyclical relevance in the early 1990s.

If it is the case that consumer trends facing the hotel industry emphasise the need for a cost-cutting approach to competitive strategy, the appropriate HRM strategy may well involve an emphasis on deskilling and routinisation. If so, then the autocratic, cost-conscious approach to the management of human resources within the industry described by Hales (1987), Lockwood and Guerrier (1989) and Macfarlane (1982) could well be a rational, strategic response to the product market contingencies facing managers within the industry.

Quality enhancement

Contrary to the opinions expressed above, many writers within the field, (Callan, 1994: 496; Haywood, 1983: 165; Kokko and Moilanen, 1997: 297; Lewis, 1987: 83; Nightingale, 1985: 9; Pye, 1994: 1) argue that, as in manufacturing, the satisfaction of evolving customer quality expectations is increasingly more important than price competition, and any hotel that does not strive to improve its service quality will lose competitiveness. As Rajan (1987: 93) states, success is increasingly dependent on awareness of consumer tastes and on quality of service. Extras, he claims, are becoming essentials.

The quality enhancement imperative is exacerbated, according to Olsen (1989: 5) by the fact that the market is reaching maturity. As the market exits its growth phase, the generation of new business becomes dependent on the ability to increase market share. This, in turn, is dependent upon the ability to provide quality and choice of service. According to Senior and Morphew (1990: 6) the competitive pressure to compete on quality does not apply to the top luxury hotels alone, but to the budget sectors also.

Service quality may well be increasingly critical to competitive success, but defining what exactly is meant by 'service quality' is somewhat more problematic. It is, according to Lewis (1987: 84), an elusive concept, which implies much more than adherence to tangible quality standards such as clean rooms, the correct number of bars of soap in the wash rooms or meals served at the right temperature. Lewis suggests that service quality exists along three dimensions. Technical quality concerns the quality of the bed and meal, for example, and functional quality concerns the quality of the service process itself. Together, these two create subjective perceptions relating to 'image', the third quality dimension. Similarly, Nightingale (1985: 10) suggests that service quality has four components, these being the quality of consumable physical goods such as the food in a restaurant, the quality of facilities, the quality of interactions with those providing the service, and finally, the quality of information about the service. Jones (1983: 93) suggests that quality should be viewed as a 'value package' or a 'benefit bundle' which includes the service and atmosphere as well as the food and beverages. Customer perceptions of quality involve the whole synergy rather than the sum of the constituent parts.

While 'service quality' might be difficult to define, it is particularly notable that within all the definitions of service quality, considerable importance is placed on the nature of the interaction between the individual employee and the customer at the point of service, in terms of politeness, overall profession-alism and the speed and thoroughness with which any problems can be addressed. As Mattsson (1994: 48) comments, the customer is inextricably linked to the provision of the service. As such, the interaction between employee and customer is a critical part of the overall service product, and critical to the customer's perception of the quality of that product.

However, ensuring a high quality interaction at the point of service is no easy task. Firstly, management cannot monitor or supervise every interaction, so much responsibility for ensuring a high quality of service has to be left to the individual contact person (Mattsson, 1994: 53). Secondly, no two service interactions are ever identical, and some customer requests may require unique responses. As such, employees have to deal with a higher degree of uncertainty within their job roles than they would do if they were working within a manufacturing environment (Schaffer, 1984: 164), and they must be capable of tailoring the service to 'suit' individual customers. Thirdly, high quality service provision represents the ultimate in 'right-first-time'. The customer expects performance of certain functions without failure, and the need to make corrective or compensating actions will detract from the overall percep-tion of quality, particularly if problems cannot be remedied quickly (Haywood 1983: 168–9). Hence, an extremely high degree of importance is attached to the job role performed by front-line staff. Indeed, the high degree of importance attached to front-line staff is emphasised within Nailon's statement that:

> any combination of technology, decor, architecture, sales promotion, management information systems or other sophisticated management techniques can be copied. The only unique asset of a commercial hospitality operation is the staff at the end of the delivery system.
>
> Nailon (1989: 77)

Mattsson (1994: 57) and Kokko and Moilanen (1997: 299) argue that front-line staff are so important that hotel organisational charts should be inverted, with the front-line employee at the top of the 'inverted pyramid', and management and all backroom functions providing support to the front-line featuring lower down the pyramid. As within the models of HRM presented by Guest (1987), Walton (1985) and Beer *et al.* (1984), front-line employees are viewed as the organisation's most important asset, being capable of achieving and sustaining competitive advantage.

However, given the uncertainty of the service delivery process, it is not possible to prescribe or routinise job tasks to ensure quality standards, as the service process must account for the potential individuality of each customer's needs, and the need to 'tailor' the service to suit individual customers. For example, scripts for waitering staff or receptionists cannot take into account the degree of complexity of customer behaviour. Similarly, quality assurances and procedures derived from manufacturing, for example BS 5750, which focus on aspects of the production process, would lead to a product rather than a service orientation – emphasising, for example, properly made up beds or clean kitchens, rather than the quality of the interaction at the point of service delivery (Callan, 1994: 486–9; Johns, 1992: 4–5). Such a focus may not necessarily address all the issues the customer sees as important.

As such, several writers within the hotel industry emphasise the importance of the development of employee commitment to service quality goals and the development of competencies to enable staff to operate more effectively within wider job roles. For example, Jones (1983: 94), Lashley (1995: 31, 1996: 344), Lefever and Reich (1991: 308), Wycott (1984) and Haywood (1983) all emphasise the development of shared values and commitment to quality enhancement. Jones (1983: 94), Lefever and Reich (1991: 308), Wycott (1984) and Haywood (1983: 166) stress the importance of communication, participation and job satisfaction. Drawing on Peters and Waterman (1982), Lefever and Reich (1991: 309–10) state that management in the industry should emphasise innovation, informality and a people orientation, rather than a cost-conscious, formal control orientation.

The emphasis on commitment, employee development and employee involvement within the hotel industry literature is clearly congruent with the human resource goals emphasised within the models of HRM presented by Guest (1987), Walton (1985) and Beer *et al.* (1984). In addition, the justifications offered concerning the importance of commitment echo those found within the HRM literature. For example, Jones and Davies (1991) argue that the development of workforce commitment to the goals of service quality is essential if authority is to be devolved to the front-line in order that problems may be dealt with at source. Committed workers are also more likely to contribute to continuous improvement processes. Indeed, because operative-level staff are in constant, close contact with customers, and as such possess a considerable amount of knowledge in relation to customer perceptions, Nightingale (1985: 18) sees their contribution to continuous improvement processes as essential. The development of workforce commitment to quality is essential if this knowledge is to be tapped effectively.

Furthermore, as within the Beer *et al.* (1984), Guest (1987) and Walton (1985) models of HRM, the development of workforce commitment is viewed within the hotel industry literature as dependent upon the introduction of a specific set of HRM practices. For example, with reference to recruitment and training, Jones (1983: 98–9) attaches importance to the careful selection of those most likely to respond to a participative management style, and also to training in social skills to enhance sensitivity to customer needs. King (1984: 92) suggests the need to screen out candidates that are unable to handle stress and to screen out candidates with a directive rather than a supportive leadership style. Mills (1986: 39–43) recommends personality testing to identify those with an ability to empathise with customers. Pye (1994: 2) stresses the importance of more sophisticated recruitment techniques to identify individuals with the appropriate 'service orientation'.

Such an approach is also seen as having major implications for management style. For example, Nightingale (1985: 9) stresses managers' participative role as facilitators and providers of information. Ross (1995) suggests that an empathetic management in the eyes of employees may lead to a more positive and contented workforce. Mattsson (1994) comments that if the right values are to be nurtured among staff, it is essential that management adopt a 'service leadership' approach. More specifically:

> …managers really should build a service climate and serve in a supportive function by inspiring and communicating high quality standards. The manager would then become more of a coach than a boss…
>
> (Mattsson, 1994: 56)

Lefever and Reich (1991: 308) argue that quality values should be taken into account in long-term strategic planning at senior management levels. This would prevent organisations from relying solely on short-term cost measures, or simply the measurable aspects of performance.

To summarise, there is a strong argument that a focus on service quality is the key to competitive advantage within the hotel industry, and also that service quality cannot be improved by task prescription and routinisation. What is needed is a well-trained and professional workforce that is committed to the achievement of quality goals. This, in turn, is dependent upon the introduction of a specific approach to HRM.

This discussion of the influence of product markets clearly demonstrates that while there is some lack of consensus concerning emerging consumer trends within the hotel industry, the nature of product markets within the hotel industry literature – as within the mainstream HRM literature – is seen as a key determinant of the approach taken to HRM.

It is also clear that a paradox exists within the hotel industry literature. The majority of writers have argued for some time that quality enhancement is the key to effectiveness. However, with the exception of a few very recent accounts, the majority of empirical studies have suggested a lack of interest in the approaches to HRM that are the most likely to support a quality enhancer strategy. This suggests a mismatch between emergent consumer trends, and both the business strategy and HRM strategy that have been adopted within the majority of hotels. One possibility is that there may be factors other than those relating to product markets that militate against the adoption of an HRM approach. Alternatively, it could be that there is nothing particularly strategic about management decision-making in the hotel industry. As discussed in the previous chapter, achieving a match between business strategy and HR strategy, and between business strategy and the product market, is by no means straightforward (Legge, 1995; Mabey and Salaman, 1995). If strategy is emergent rather than planned for example, or where HR lacks boardroom representation, such a mismatch becomes a possibility. The next section looks firstly at this likelihood, and then at other factors that might militate against the adoption of HRM within the industry.

How 'strategic' is management in the hotel industry?

Is it the case that managers in the hotel industry systematically analyse the product market in which their hotel operates, and then adopt a business strategy and the HR strategy most appropriate to that market analysis? Probably not, according to Haywood (1983: 170), who claims there to be a widespread belief within the industry that managers are able to identify intuitively causes of customer dissatisfaction and rectify them immediately. Haywood continues by suggesting that unless formal techniques such as quality audits are used to discover customer perceptions of service quality, management will tend to focus on the tangible, more controllable aspects of the service such as cleanliness, rather than on less measurable aspects such as staff politeness. The implication of his argument is that as few hotels operate systematic mechanisms by which managers can find out what customers view as important, the development of a customer-oriented business strategy driven by customer preferences is unlikely.

Supporting this view, Guerrier and Lockwood (1989a: 82–3), claim that management in the industry reflects a 'hands on', 'operational' perspective, characterised by a preference for dealing with real 'live' problems, and a focus on day-to-day functioning and short time horizons, rather than a reflective 'business perspective' approach, characterised by strategic thought on how to best develop the business. It would seem therefore that conscious, planned business strategy-making does not figure much within the industry. In such a situation, as described by Legge (1995), the link between product markets, business strategy and HR strategy will be lost. It is highly unlikely that the appropriate HR strategy will emerge where managers in the first instance have failed to identify the business strategy appropriate to emerging market trends.

Why the focus on operational issues, and a lack of a 'business perspective', as described by Guerrier and Lockwood (1989a)? One view is that there are shortfalls in terms of management training. The management apprenticeship system has tended to emphasise the operational rather than strategic aspects of hotel management. Trainee managers, moving between hotels to gain experience in a number of fields, find themselves dealing with consecutive operational crises, never having the opportunity to analyse the root cause of problems. Thus, the skills developed tend to be those necessary to deal with operational issues – such as how to carve salmon – rather than the skills necessary to deal with business-related issues such as how to use a spreadsheet or develop a marketing plan (Guerrier and Lockwood, 1989a: 84).

As a solution, several writers urge for greater attention to be paid to management training and development. For example, Kelliher and Johnson (1987: 107) state that management should be made more conscious of the potential contribution of the personnel function and that those involved in personnel management should be trained in the relevant skills. Similarly, Kane (1986: 51) claims that training in the proper application of personnel management is essential to reduce the industry's chronic productivity and job satisfaction problems. Haywood (1983: 170) suggests that training managers in the use of quality audits would help to address shortcomings relating to strategic business planning. A quality audit, Haywood claims, would reveal the complexity and volatility of the service process. Managers would realise that a focus on cost control would fail to meet customer expectations, and they would subsequently realise the need for a responsive and empowered workforce.

Is it realistic, however, to argue that management training in quality audits and in the application of certain personnel or HRM techniques will have much of an impact? As previously noted, Guerrier and Lockwood (1989a: 82) argue that hotel management tends to be 'hands on' with an emphasis on dealing with real 'live' problems and operating on short time horizons rather than taking a long-term reflective approach. This situation has developed over time from traditional hotel industry organisational culture, in particular, managers' traditional roles as welcoming hosts. This, in turn, has led to a culture that over-emphasises the importance of front-of-house and food and beverage functions, and the importance of being seen to 'be there' (Guerrier and Lockwood, 1989a). This bias within management culture itself militates against the adoption of a more business-oriented approach, as the prevailing culture dictates that it is more important to be seen to be dealing with short-term operational difficulties personally, rather than to be concerned with longer-term business development. Breaking away from this culture will be difficult. Managers have some degree of choice as to how they define their roles, but those who get on careerwise tend to be those who define their roles as the senior management sees fit (Guerrier and Lockwood, 1989a: 83). If the hotel's management style is 'hands on', then there will be pressure on junior managers to follow suit, and mimic the management style of their superiors, irrespective of skills learned in an off-the-job classroom or college training situation. The effective introduction of a business-oriented approach would therefore involve a questioning of some of the fundamental aspects of existing management style, and would require a significant cultural change throughout the entire organisation (Guerrier and Lockwood, 1989a: 88).

Therefore, blaming a lack of management training for a lack of interest in HRM, or suggesting that improvements can be made if managers are trained in HRM techniques, overlooks the fact that traditional approaches to management would have to change at every level throughout the organisation. Whereas this does not mean that change is impossible, the fact that such thoroughgoing change in management style would be necessary is perhaps a further reason why interest in HRM is so limited. Managers would have to be very confident that such a major upheaval in style and culture in the short-term would pay dividends in the future.

Therefore, if management in the industry is, as suggested by Guerrier and Lockwood (1989a), characterised by a concern for operational issues, it is quite possible that managers are unaware of what their customers see as important in terms of quality of service, and even if management are aware of a need for a greater emphasis on service quality, it may be the case that they are unaware of the approaches to HRM required to achieve it, or are prevented from experimenting by entrenched management styles. There is a strong argument therefore, that even where product market contingencies suggest the applicability of an HRM approach, managers themselves present a stumbling block to its introduction.

Therefore, as within the mainstream HRM literature, issues relating to the strategy-making process and the ability of management to handle change are seen as highly influential in determining the likely development of HRM within the hotel industry. There is clear common ground between the HRM literature and the hotel industry literature on these issues.

Nature and influence of the personnel department

The existence of a well-developed personnel function is a precursor for the introduction of HRM, as argued by Guest and Hoque (1994a) and Marginson *et al.* (1993) within the mainstream literature. Within the hotel industry, there is an increasing consensus that the number of personnel specialists is much higher than has previously been acknowledged. Boella (1986: 30) estimates that prior to the 1963 Contracts of Employment Act, there were only about 20 personnel managers in the UK hotel industry. The profession began to grow following the introduction of the Act, which required employers to provide written terms and conditions and pay records. The 1970s, according to Boella (1986) saw a growth in the number of personnel specialists and a growth in the number of boardroom personnel specialists in the industry. During the 1980s, a maturing process took place, with the number of specialist personnel managers in the industry, many of whom had experience of personnel management elsewhere, continuing to rise.

The available empirical evidence increasingly supports Boella's argument, at least with reference to the number of personnel specialists within the industry. For example, Lucas (1996), using data from the third Workplace Industrial Relations Survey (WIRS3), found that within hotels and catering, there was a higher incidence of either a manager responsible for personnel issues or a specialist personnel manager than in other parts of the trading sector. Managers responsible for personnel were also better qualified and were more likely to be supported by a team of back-up staff. Similarly, Price (1994) found the same proportion of the hotels within her sample to have a specialist as within WIRS3, and that the hotel industry specialists were equally well qualified.

Other surveys also suggest that the number of personnel specialists within the industry has increased. Kelliher and Johnson (1987) found that while the presence of a specialist was related heavily to size, 96 per cent of hotels with 200 rooms or more had a personnel specialist plus back-up team. By contrast, only 14 per cent of establishments with 100 rooms or less had a personnel specialist. In a follow-up survey conducted a decade later, looking at hotels with 150 rooms or more, they found 88 per cent of establishments to have a full-time member of staff responsible for personnel matters (Kelliher and Johnson, 1997).

While there is significant agreement relating to the extent to which the number of specialist personnel managers has risen within the hotel industry, there is a higher degree of debate over the extent to which those personnel specialists are likely to potentially champion the introduction of HRM. Price (1994) suggests that despite the evidence of a growth in the number of personnel specialists, there remains a worrying lack of basic professionalism in the conduct of personnel management. Similarly, Lucas (1996) argues that despite the apparently high degree of personnel specialists, the industry continues to suffer poor industrial relations outcomes, relating to quit rates, recourse to the grievance procedure and the rate of dismissals. The role of personnel specialists in the industry may have more to do with the administration of these activities than with the development of more sophisticated approaches to HRM.

However, other studies paint a more positive picture. Kelliher and Johnson (1987) originally drew similar conclusions to those reached by Price (1994), though the evidence within their follow-up survey (Kelliher and Johnson, 1997) suggests that personnel departments within the industry have become increasingly sophisticated. In their earlier study, they found that half of the respondents had never had any previous personnel experience. Most had worked their way up through line management, their knowledge of personnel being acquired on the job. Only one respondent had an Institute of Personnel Management (IPM) qualification. There was a great deal of reliance on personnel instruction manuals, issued by head office, which did not allow for adaptation to local contingencies. As such, personnel departments were found to be somewhat reactive and inflexible.

Kelliher and Johnson (1987) also found personnel department activities to be narrowly defined. Seventy-one per cent of respondents saw recruitment as being their key responsibility, simply getting enough staff to fill jobs in response to high turnover. Sixty-three per cent also identified training as a key responsibility, once again, in response to high levels of labour turnover. Of other possible areas of responsibility, only welfare and maintenance of staff records featured to any extent. The conclusion was therefore reached that on the whole, personnel management was not taken seriously in the industry, with many hotels, particularly the smaller ones, simply 'dumping' the function on a line manager.

In the follow-up survey, however, Kelliher and Johnson (1997) found considerable evidence of an increased level of sophistication. The update showed that while head offices continued to keep tight control over the activities of individual units, there was evidence of adaptation at local level of initiatives fed down from above. Moreover, 60 per cent of respondents now reported involvement in budget setting and involvement in mainstream business decision-making. Kelliher and Johnson (1997) therefore concluded within their more recent survey that personnel management within the hotel industry has developed into a mainstream business activity, and also that personnel specialists are now involved in a wider range of activities than before.

There is therefore considerable debate over the extent to which personnel managers are likely to champion the introduction of a more sophisticated approach to HRM. The nature of the personnel department, seen as an important influence on the approach taken to HRM in the mainstream literature, is also viewed as an important influence within the hotel industry.

In a sense, it is easy to blame management for the apparent failure to innovate in terms of HRM. It is managers who have the resources and authority to experiment with more innovative approaches, yet they seem to lack the ability, knowledge or willingness to do so. However, managers have to deal with a range of possible influences that might restrict their freedom to experiment with HRM initiatives. These influences will now be considered in turn.

Variable nature of demand

It is commonly argued that because demand for the hotel industry product is inherently seasonal, high numbers of temporary and casual workers are required. This problem is worsened by the fact that it is not possible to hold stock to meet future demand, as would be the case in manufacturing (Haywood,

1983: 169). Smoothing out staffing levels by continuing production levels in slack times and holding stock until the market picks up, as typically happened in the UK car industry in the lead up to the August sales peak, for example, is not an option in hotels. As a result, there is a greater urgency to match staffing levels to variations in demand. The potential cost savings to be made from the strategic management of casuals, temporary workers and part-time workers is considerable, as found by Walsh (1991: 107), using data from nine case studies. The productivity enhancement arising from a 'just-in-time' flexible labour utilisation, should not, Walsh concludes, be underestimated.

There is obviously a trade-off. Employing large numbers of staff on non-standard contracts and granting them little in terms of job security or career prospects will inevitably impact on workforce commitment and adherence to quality goals. As Guerrier and Lockwood (1989b: 15) state, it is important to get the core/periphery mix right in order to enable quality to remain a central focus while simultaneously enabling costs to be minimised. Nevertheless, if the gains to be made from the strategic use of temporary and part-time workers are as high as Walsh (1991) claims, managers would have to be very confident that the additional costs involved in offering greater stability of employment would pay dividends in the long term.

This argument, however, rests on the extent to which demand is indeed variable. While there will inevitably be variations in the demand for labour during the course of the day, there is greater debate over the extent to which demand in the hotel industry follows a seasonal pattern. Inevitably, where demand is seasonal, a high proportion of the workforce will be on temporary contracts. However, Shamir (1978: 302) argues that the proportion of hotel conference business is increasing, and because such business lacks a cyclical pattern, demand is stabilising. Hence, within hotels dependent for a sizeable proportion of their trade on business customers, seasonality becomes less of an issue where HRM policy choice is concerned. The extent of the impact of seasonality of demand on the approach taken to HRM is therefore by no means a foregone conclusion.

Workforce resistance to change

Guest (1987) makes the point that workforce resistance to change will impede the introduction of HRM. Similarly, within the hotel industry, the amenability of the workforce to change, and whether or not that amenability would stretch to an acceptance of HRM practices, is open to question. For example, Guerrier and Lockwood (1989c) found staff to be favourable towards the idea of flexibility as long as it was not downwards. Similarly, research by Mars, Bryant and Mitchell (1979), quoted in Wood (1992: 143), showed that multi-skilling could work, though it required the recruitment of fresh labour. Wood (1992: 146) also believes that there is scope for functional flexibility where chambermaids are concerned, in that they can be given autonomy over their own set of rooms and made responsible for their own quality. Shamir (1978: 304) notes that multi-skilling in the form of the 'hostess' system, within which a single employee acts as receptionist, chambermaid and waitress for a group of customers, has been experimented with successfully in some hotels.

However, there is also considerable evidence to suggest that any change in working arrangements would be met by possibly insurmountable resistance from existing entrenched working practices and patterns of industrial relations. Macfarlane (1982: 37), quoting the Commission on Industrial Relations (1971), states that, quite often, departments within hotels operate on the basis that other parts of the hotel do not exist. Supporting this argument, in their two case study hotels, Guerrier and Lockwood (1989c: 412–13) found that because considerable authority had been decentralised to individual departments, all of which had been designated as individual cost centres, front- and back-of-house functions developed a strong sense of attachment to their skills, occupational identity and distinct sub-cultures. For example, staff in the sport and fitness centre had little interest in the running of the rest of the hotel. As a result, it was difficult to foster any sense of cross-functional flexibility.

Although Wood (1992: 143, 146) notes potential for the multi-skilling of chambermaids, he is less optimistic where other occupations are concerned, many of which are characterised by rigidly adhered to status divisions. For example in the kitchen and dining areas, the head waiter is junior to the head chef, but is senior to a junior chef. Wood (1992: 52–60) also comments on conflict both within and between departments. Within departments, conflict is most likely where jobs are tippable. Wood (1992: 57) provides examples of waitresses hiding equipment, in order that they may rectify the 'mistakes' made by other waitresses, and hence maximise their likelihood of a tip. Friction between jobs that are tippable and those that are not is also likely, the classic example being between waiters and chefs. Chefs are put under pressure for speedy service from waiters, but they are conscious of the fact that this pressure is a result of waiters wishing to maximise their tips. Further examples of conflict between departments include the potential for resentment towards receptionists owing to their ability to generate work for other departments such as housekeeping, maintenance and portering. Such conflict is unlikely to prove conducive to team development and cross-functional flexibility.

Further potential for workforce resistance to change is generated by the informal contracts that tend to develop between individual employees and their direct superiors. Wood (1992: 47–51), drawing on work undertaken by Mars and Mitchell (1976), argues that the practice of pilferage and petty theft, which is rife throughout the industry, is tolerated within limits. Indeed, management has an interest in maintaining these relationships, as if the need arises to reduce headcount, it is possible to do so quickly and cheaply, simply by selecting for dismissal those known to engage in such activities. In this manner, redundancy payments or lengthy notice periods can be avoided. Naturally, the workforce also has an interest in such relationships, seeing pilferage as a normal part of remuneration. There is, therefore, potential for resistance to the introduction of HRM initiatives if they are likely to result in an erosion of informal contracts. Any reform to pay systems, or attempt to reform workplace culture that might break the informal contract between supervisor and employee or might result in the supervisor removing his or her endorsement of pilferage, would be seen by the employee as a worsening of terms and conditions. What is more, resistance is likely to be strongest from the organisation's core employees, as it is they who are the most likely to have developed an informal contract with their supervisor, and hence will experience the larger debit effect.

Thus, as argued within the mainstream literature, there are considerable grounds to argue that certain entrenched custom and practice may result in workforce resistance to the introduction of new style working arrangements. While Wood (1992: 60) concedes that such problems are not unique to the hotel industry, he states that they are too institutionalised simply to be solved by better management.

Workplace size

As emphasised within the HRM models presented by Hendry and Pettigrew (1986, 1990), workplace size is viewed as an important influence on the approach taken to HRM within the hotel industry. Site location within the industry is governed by consumer demands, so it is not possible to distribute the hotel product from a centralised unit, as tends to happen in the manufacturing sector (Mullins, 1993: 5). As a result, the industry is dominated by small establishments (Price, 1994), within which communication and consultation relies on face-to-face contact between owners and staff, rather than on formal HRM procedures. Admittedly, there are small firms in manufacturing where the same principle applies, but the proportion of small firms is greater in the hotel industry. Formal HRM policies are therefore inappropriate to a larger proportion of the industry.

However, this does not mean that HRM is irrelevant in larger hotels. For example, Price (1994) found that larger hotels were improving their personnel practices and increasingly realising the need for training. Also, HRM may hold greater relevance within hotel chains. While not disputing that the actual size of individual units is smaller in the hotel industry than in manufacturing, Shamir (1978: 303) argues that hotel chains are accounting for an increasingly large proportion of the total market. Chains need to adopt a consistency between workplaces in order that standardisation may be sold as a guarantee of quality. As such, they are more likely to take a formal approach to HR planning, as senior managers implement rules and regulations, and 'best practice' manuals in order to standardise employee behaviour across the chain.

Workforce instability and labour turnover

According to Wood (1992: 95), there is general agreement concerning the level of turnover in the industry. Commonly quoted figures are an industry average of 70 per cent, though unit rates as high as 300 per cent are not uncommon. In Johnson's (1985) study of ten hotels, he found that labour turnover was 75 per cent on average, down from 125 per cent five years earlier. Johnson put this down to the higher level of unemployment, hence fewer alternative employment opportunities, at the time of the second survey. Either figure demonstrates a level of labour turnover that is much higher than within the rest of the economy, within which turnover is in the region of 14 per cent, according to WIRS3 (Millward *et al.*, 1992). It seems therefore that the problem of high turnover is in many respects unique to the hotel industry.

It is likely that high levels of labour turnover will have a potentially detrimental impact on attempts to adopt an HRM approach. As Nailon (1989: 77) suggests, employment stability is essential if shared values are to develop. He states:

> The achievement of excellence takes time, not only for thinking and planning. Stability is therefore requisite in that both manager and staff

must work together over a significant period of time to establish quality, consistency and guaranteed standards...

The stability that Nailon suggests is so important is lacking in the vast majority of hotels in the UK.

However, there is considerable debate as to whether it is possible to reduce the labour turnover that exist within the UK hotel industry. Several writers argue that turnover can be reduced by better management. For example, Johnson (1985) suggests that turnover may be the result of management inability to monitor occupancy, overtime levels and staff departures. This finding is corroborated by Macauley and Wood (1992: 48) who likewise attribute very high levels of labour turnover in their study to miscalculations in manpower planning. Therefore, the implication is that if manpower planning were to improve, rates of turnover would decrease. Denvir and McMahon (1992: 147) suggest that labour turnover in the industry can be reduced considerably if management create an environment that fosters the retention of high quality staff. Lefever and Reich (1991: 308) suggest that turnover can be reduced by 'surfacing' the values of the organisation at an early stage within the recruitment process. Ohlin and West (1994) suggest that fringe benefits and retirement programmes can help reduce turnover, though Iverson and Deery (1997) suggest that mechanisms such as improved internal labour markets, job security, career development and promotion opportunities are likely to prove more effective. Indeed, Wood and Macauley (1989) found hotels that had developed supervisory and management development programmes and a 'hire from within' policy to have reduced turnover.

However, others argue that studies suggesting labour turnover would be reduced if the industry were to be made a more attractive employment prospect, ignore the real facts of hotel life. Referring to studies by Mars, Bryant and Mitchell (1979) and Shamir (1981), Wood (1992: 17–25) describes workers in the hotel industry as 'non-conforming', 'nomadic' and dishonest delinquents, who are psychologically and socially marginalised. Shamir (1981) suggests that the practice of 'living-in' adds to instability by attracting unstable, marginal groups to the industry, for example, foreigners looking for free accommodation, young people looking for the opportunity to leave home and those with broken marriages. 'Living-in' further adds to instability by making moves between workplaces easier. Transience is also generated by split shifts, which result in workers being present within the workplace while not on duty, hence contributing to feelings of a need for a change of scene. High guest mobility also increases feelings of transience. Given the inherent instability of the industry's workforce,

Wood (1992: 23) concludes that it is overly optimistic to suggest that labour turnover can be overcome by practices aimed at the encouragement of employee retention.

Moreover, there is considerable debate over the extent to which labour turnover is in fact dysfunctional. Johnson (1985) found management to be happy with high levels of labour turnover, as it enables them to shed inefficient staff and to reduce headcount quickly and easily. However, he still concludes that high turnover leads to high replacement and training costs, and lower quality staff lacking firm-specific human capital. Denvir and McMahon (1992: 143) argue that a high turnover rate, which is a pointer to satisfaction and morale problems, leads to compromised standards, poor productivity, reduced quality of staff and a reduced stock of skills. Similarly, Iverson and Deery (1997: 80) argue that turnover dramatically increases costs and reduces service quality.

By contrast, Riley (1993) argues that given the peaky nature of demand for hotel services, labour turnover is a crucial mechanism that enables management to deal with fluctuating manpower needs. Using labour turnover for this purpose also encourages management to adopt a deskilling strategy, as it is easier to manipulate the manpower levels of unskilled workers than skilled workers. Thus, the cost-cutting potential of labour turnover is twofold. Firstly, it provides a mechanism by which variations in demand for labour can be dealt with. Secondly, by encouraging deskilling, it enables pay levels to be kept to a minimum.

There is therefore considerable debate over the likely impact of labour turnover in the industry. It is seen by some as inevitable, and not necessarily problematic. Given the cost-control potential of labour turnover, and given the doubt as to whether it can be reduced anyway, it is not surprising, as Wood (1992: 103) argues, that most managers in the hotel industry do not view it as a problem. Within such a context, where high labour turnover is viewed as a fact of life, there is little scope for the effective application of HRM. By contrast, others view turnover as damaging to service quality, yet reducible via better management and the introduction of HRM practices.

Either way, this debate is in many respects unique to the hotel industry, with turnover not being viewed as a major influence on HRM policy within the mainstream literature. According to WIRS3, turnover is in the region of 14 per cent (Millward *et al.*, 1992) for the economy as a whole. The extent to which turnover influences management decision-making is therefore an important test of the extent to which the hotel industry is 'different' from industries elsewhere.

Workforce skill levels

Within the mainstream HRM literature, Keep (1989) argues that Britain's training record acts as a serious hindrance to the adoption of new approaches to HRM. Within the hotel industry, Prais, Jarvis and Wagner (1989) found a lack of vocational training in UK hotels in comparison with hotels in Germany. This was instrumental in explaining the differences in labour productivity within the hotels studied in the two countries. It would be sensible to hypothesise that, as multi-skilling and functional flexibility are likely to feature as key HR goals, a lack of skills training will militate against the adoption of HRM within the industry, as it is seen to do within the mainstream HRM literature.

Trade unions

Trade union density within the hotel industry is extremely low, and, as such, the impact of unions on management decision-making is likely to be minimal. According to WIRS3 (Millward, *et al.* 1992) trade union density is 3 per cent in the hotel industry, with unions recognised in only 8 per cent of establishments. The low level of unionisation is partly explained by the high proportion of seasonal and part-time workers within the industry, though Wood (1992: 104–5) points out further reasons why recruitment within the industry is particularly difficult. Firstly, the practice of tipping has generated an ethos of individualism and instrumentalism, which in turn, detracts from workforce cohesion. Secondly, the industry is isolated from wider working class influences. For example, 'living-in' isolates the employee from dichotomous views of class society. Also, the close working relationships which often develop between employees and guests, who are on the whole of a higher social status than employees, tend to result in a desire among employees to emulate, or to identify with superiors, rather than to identify with working-class goals. Finally, the industry is characterised by the existence of numerous small units. The resulting geographical dispersion of the industry makes recruitment difficult. To date, the unions have failed to develop solutions to deal with these issues.

While there is considerable debate over the impact of trade unions on the approach taken to HRM within the mainstream literature (see for example Guest, 1995; Trades Union Congress, 1994), little has been written expressly on the impact of unions on HRM in the hotel industry. Nevertheless, while unions are unlikely to influence management decision-making (Lucas, 1996), the non-union nature of the industry is worthy of further discussion. A combination of the lack of trade unions in the industry and the marginality of the hotel industry workforce could encourage exploitation and work intensification rather than the introduction of HRM. If unions held more influence within the industry, then managers might be encouraged to adopt a 'best practice' approach as it would not be possible to achieve productivity gains via work intensification, or cost savings via low pay. Conversely, should managers wish to experiment with innovative approaches to HRM, they will not be hindered by union resistance (Gilbert and Guerrier, 1997: 122).

While the lack of trade unions in the industry will inevitably give management a considerable degree of freedom in terms of the approach to HRM they choose to adopt, it is not the case that the non-union nature of the hotel industry contributes to the industry's uniqueness. Firstly, much of the HRM literature is written from a unitarist perspective, and in the case of Walton (1985), virtually makes an assumption of non-unionism. Secondly, trade union density in the UK currently stands at around 30 per cent, and within the private sector, only one in five workers belongs to a trade union. The hotel industry is, if anything, part of the rule on this issue, rather than the exception.

Foreign ownership

Much has been written in recent years on the HRM practices adopted within high-profile manufacturing inward investors, and about the effectiveness of the approaches they have adopted. There is evidence that British companies have attempted to emulate the success of their overseas counterparts also. Whether such demonstration effects exist within the hotel industry remains open to question. Nevertheless, Price (1994) claims that the foreign-owned hotels within her sample appear to have developed a more professional approach towards personnel management than have British-owned hotels. Others demonstrate similar findings (Lucas and Laycock, 1991).

If foreign-owned hotels have indeed been more successful in adopting a sophisticated approach, this has several implications. Firstly, as pointed out by Price (1994), the best graduates from hotel and catering colleges will not be attracted to British hotel chains. Secondly, if there is a relationship between HRM and performance, British hotels will lose out in terms of competitiveness to their foreign rivals. It is of paramount importance therefore to establish both the nature of HRM in foreign-owned hotels and also the nature of the relationship between HRM and performance. It is clear that the issue of national ownership, seen as important within the mainstream HRM literature particularly in relation to the Japanisation debate, is also an issue of considerable importance within the hotel industry.

Conclusions and discussion

This chapter highlights a range of potential influences on HRM policy choice in the hotel industry. Debates concerning the appropriate competitive response to emerging consumer trends, workforce or management receptiveness to change, the strategic capacity of management to handle change, fluctuations in patterns of demand, organisational aspects of the industry such as establishment size, workforce instability and national ownership highlight the differences in opinion which exist concerning the potential role of HRM in the industry. There are compelling arguments suggesting that HRM has a potential contribution to make, but equally compelling arguments that its role will always be restricted. Subsequent chapters will test the extent to which the factors discussed here either encourage or restrict the adoption of HRM in the industry.

One thing that is clear, however, is that there are key similarities between the debates in the hotel industry literature and debates in the HRM literature, in relation to the factors that are likely to influence the approach taken to HRM. Firstly, as within the mainstream HRM literature, product markets within the hotel industry are seen as a key determinant of business strategy and as a key determinant of HRM policy choice. The Schuler and Jackson (1987) model seems particularly relevant given that, in line with the key differences of opinion within the hotel industry, it emphasises cost reduction and quality enhancement as alternative approaches to business strategy. Moreover, both Schuler and Jackson (1987) within the mainstream literature and also Kokko and Moilanen (1997: 299), Lefever and Reich (1991: 308) and Mattsson (1994: 57) within the hotel industry literature suggest the HR strategy appropriate to quality enhancement to be one of high commitment. Conversely, where cost reducer business strategies are concerned, both sets of literature suggest the use of non-standard labour and deskilling to be the appropriate HR responses.

Secondly, the conflicting interpretations of changing market trends within the industry offered by Callan (1994), Haywood (1983), Kokko and Moilanen (1997), Larmour (1983), Lewis (1987), Nightingale (1985) and Shamir (1978) bear a resemblance to the conflicting viewpoints offered by Piore and Sabel (1984) and Pollert (1991). Whether consumers really are coming to demand higher quality, customised and personalised products, underpins the debate over the applicability of the Beer *et al.* (1984), Guest (1987) and Walton (1985) approaches to HRM, and the extent to which these models can be viewed as universally relevant. In the hotel industry literature, Callan (1994), Haywood (1983), Kokko and Moilanen (1997), Lewis (1987), Nightingale (1985) and Pye (1994) offer an interpretation not dissimilar from Piore and

Sabel (1982) and Walton (1985), arguing that consumer trends are indeed coming to reflect the need for higher quality, and as such the appropriate approach to HRM is to try to increase workforce commitment. By contrast, Larmour (1983) and Shamir (1978) argue, in a similar vein to Pollert (1991), that consumer trends have not undergone such dramatic change in recent times, and as such, HRM is not necessarily any more appropriate in the industry today than at any time in the past.

Turning to the debates relating to workforce characteristics, further similarities between the hotel industry literature and the mainstream HRM literature can be identified. Guest (1987) sees entrenched working practices as one explanation behind the low take-up of HRM. This issue is accorded a considerable degree of importance by Guerrier and Lockwood (1989a), Wood (1992: 143, 146) and Macfarlane (1982) within the hotel industry. In addition, arguments similar to those made by Sisson and Storey (1990) as well as Guest (1987), relating to the inability of management to be able to handle strategic change, are raised by Guerrier and Lockwood (1989a) and Haywood (1983) within the hotel industry literature. The impact of unionisation, or the lack of unions in the case of the hotel industry is discussed by Gilbert and Guerrier (1997) and Lucas (1996). Concerns relating to the level of vocational skills training as raised by Keep (1989) within the mainstream HRM literature, are voiced by Prais, Jarvis and Wagner (1989) with reference to the hotel industry. Foreign ownership is also considered by Lucas and Laycock (1991) and Price (1994) to be an important influence on the approach taken to HRM. Finally, issues within the mainstream literature relating to workplace characteristics are also considered important within the hotel industry. Price's (1994) arguments relating to establishment size, and Shamir's (1978) arguments relating to hotel chains, are not dissimilar to those discussed within Hendry and Pettigrew's (1986, 1990) HRM framework.

Indeed, the only influences on HRM that can be considered unique to the hotel industry are labour turnover and instability of demand, and there is considerable debate over the likely impact of these factors anyway. The only major influence on HRM discussed within the mainstream HRM literature that fails to receive attention within the hotel industry literature concerns the impact of financial markets and decentralisation, as discussed by Kirkpatrick, Davies and Oliver (1992) and Purcell (1989: 73). It would be reasonable therefore to conclude that there is considerable common ground between the influences on HRM seen as important within the hotel industry and the influences on management seen as important elsewhere. This is an important test of the relevance of HRM theory in the hotel industry. There is little to suggest that the factors likely to influence decision-making in relation to HRM within the industry are hugely different from the factors that are likely to influence decision-making in other industries. Hence, there is little to suggest that the hotel industry is really any 'different' from industries elsewhere, and there are no reasons why theoretical propositions developed within the mainstream HRM literature, though developed within a manufacturing paradigm, should be considered inapplicable to the industry.

A further issue raised by this chapter concerns what exactly is meant by 'best practice' HRM in the context of the hotel industry. There are currently several grey areas. Little is said on pay mechanisms, for example whether a merit pay system linked to performance appraisal would be appropriate. There is likewise little on job design or on training. Perhaps more importantly, little is said on how shared values can be achieved when levels of pay are so low. Teare and Brotherton (1991) are pretty well alone in explicitly suggesting that terms and conditions, career structure, salaries and benefits are in need of improvement. Focusing attention on the implementation of methods of employee involvement, for example, may have the effect of deflecting attention away from more costly issues relating to improvements in basic pay and conditions. Furthermore, most of the literature supporting the usage of HRM in the hotel industry focuses on front-line staff coming into direct contact with customers. Yet little is said about HRM in relation to back-office staff who are not in direct contact roles. Addressing these issues will enable a more sophisticated description of what exactly is meant by 'best practice' HRM in the context of the hotel industry.

Finally, irrespective of influences on HRM policy choice, this chapter also highlights the emerging debate over the extent to which hotels have implemented practices associated with an HRM approach. Anastassova and Purcell (1995), Buick and Muthu (1997), Harrington and Akehurst (1996) and Watson and D'Annunzio-Green (1996) present primarily anecdotal accounts of HRM in practice in the hotel industry. By contrast, Lucas (1995), Price (1994) and Teare (1996) argue that there is still little to suggest that more sophisticated approaches to HRM are being adopted.

The next chapter looks at this issue, by first introducing the empirical underpinnings of the book, namely the 1995 Survey of HRM in the Hotel Industry, and then, from a comparative perspective, considering the extent to which there has been an adoption of HRM within the industry.

3 New approaches to HRM in the hotel industry[1]

A comparative analysis

As discussed within the previous chapter, considerable debate has developed concerning the extent to which there has been experimentation with HRM in the hotel industry in recent years. To recap briefly, the hotel industry has conventionally been characterised as dominated by practices aimed at an enhancement of managerial prerogative and cost reduction, and a predominance of authoritarian management styles. Empirical analyses have typically supported this characterisation. For example, Hales (1987) found a general perception amongst hotel industry managers that non-managerial employees did not want greater responsibility. Guerrier and Lockwood (1989b) and Lucas (1993) report a high level of short-term and part-time working. Prais, Jarvis and Wagner (1989) found a lack of vocational training in the hotel industry. Price (1994: 52) concludes from her research that there remains a worrying lack of basic professionalism in personnel practice. Lucas (1995: 90) and Teare (1996) argue that there is little evidence to suggest that any kind of HRM approach is being followed, even among larger organisations.

However, some recent studies have suggested that experimentation with new approaches to HRM is becoming increasingly common. For example, Harrington and Akehurst (1996) find that hotels are taking service quality more seriously. Anastassova and Purcell (1995) find evidence to suggest that hotels are adopting a more consultative management style. Buick and Muthu (1997) suggest that hotels are increasingly developing internal labour markets and career structures. Gilbert and Guerrier (1997: 122) argue that managers have taken on board notions of empowerment and teamworking and the need to devolve responsibility to lower levels. When compared with the conclusions reached by Lucas (1995), Teare (1996) and Price (1994), and also with the conclusions reached within the research undertaken during the 1980s, it becomes apparent that increasing debate over the extent to which HRM has taken hold within the hotel industry has emerged.

There is also increasing debate over the extent of development of the personnel profession. An increasing number of studies suggest that a relatively high number of personnel specialists now operate within the industry. For example, both Lucas (1995, 1996) and Price (1994) find personnel specialists to be more in evidence in the hotel and catering sectors than elsewhere. They also find specialists within the industry to be better qualified than personnel managers in other sectors of the economy. There is, however, some debate over the role of personnel specialists within the industry. Past research has tended to identify a lack of strategy and professionalism within unit-level personnel departments (for example, Guerrier and Lockwood, 1989a: 82–3; Kelliher and Johnson, 1987). Lucas (1995, 1996) suggests that their presence may have more to do with the consequences of high labour turnover rather than the development of a more strategic HRM approach. By contrast, Kelliher and Johnson (1997) argue that personnel departments have become increasingly strategic and influential within management decision-making processes.

The aim of this chapter is to shed light on the debates relating to the extent of adoption of HRM within the industry and also the extent of development of the personnel function, but to do so from a comparative perspective. The analysis here therefore not only looks at the extent to which HRM practices have been adopted within a sample of hotel industry establishments, but also tests whether the usage of the practices asked about is any more widely reported within a sample of manufacturing sector establishments. To date, such a comparative approach has rarely been used. Indeed, research undertaken by Lucas (1995, 1996) constitutes the only systematically conducted, in-depth comparative analyses of the industry. Earlier studies have looked at hotels in isolation and have inferred from the results that the industry is lagging in terms of innovation and professionalism. However, without comparing directly the extent to which HRM has been adopted within the hotel industry with the extent to which it has been adopted elsewhere, such conclusions will always be subject to a degree of uncertainty. If it can be demonstrated that hotels have shown less of an interest in HRM than have manufacturing establishments, and that they treat HR issues in a less strategic manner, considerable weight will be added to the bleak conclusions presented by Lucas (1995, 1996), Price (1994) and Teare (1996).

This chapter tests this issue by analysing data from two questionnaire-based surveys. The first, conducted in June–July 1995, collected data on a sample of hotels. The second, conducted in May–June 1993, collected similar data on a sample of greenfield-site manufacturing establishments. The establishments within both samples were asked the same set of questions about their HRM policies and practices. Combining the two surveys yields a dataset that enables a direct like-with-like analysis of the reported usage of HR practices adopted within the hotel industry in comparison with manufacturing, and a similar comparative analysis of issues relating to HR strategy. The data also enable an examination of the nature and extent of development of the personnel department within the hotel industry from a comparative perspective.

The hotels within the sample are all large by industry standards, having on average 124.95 employees (in comparison with 235.39 employees in the 1993 manufacturing sample). In addition, almost 82 per cent of the hotels within the sample are part of a chain (see Table 3.1). The sample is therefore patently unrepresentative of the industry as a whole, given that 81 per cent of hotels employ fewer than 25 people (Department of National Heritage, 1996). However, focusing on a sample of large hotels makes sense where the study of HRM is concerned, as it is only within larger establishments, hotel or otherwise, that an interest in HRM would be expected. Given the large proportion of small establishments within the hotel industry, it would come as no surprise to find levels of interest in HRM to be low within the industry as a whole. However, the more convincing test, which would provide support for the bleak scenario presented by Lucas (1995), Teare (1996) and Price (1994), would be to consider whether there is a higher reported usage of HRM within manufacturing establishments than within hotels of a comparable size, as it is amongst these establishments that an interest in HRM might be expected.

The results achieved within this analysis should be of interest not only to those with a primary research focus on the hotel industry, but also to those with a broader interest in HRM. Firstly, as discussed in the first chapter, HRM has its roots firmly entrenched within a manufacturing paradigm. However, given that almost 76 per cent of the population now work within the service sector, the future credibility of HRM is dependent upon its relevance within the services. By examining the extent to which there has been an acceptance of HRM within one part of the services, the analysis here sheds light on this issue.

Secondly, the extent to which companies within the UK have adopted HRM as encapsulated within the models presented by Guest (1987), Walton (1985) and Beer *et al.* (1984), remains very much open to question. For example, Wood and Albanese (1995) conclude that we can now speak of a 'high commitment management on the shopfloor'. However, Sisson (1993), discussing HRM with reference to WIRS3, argues that only 'fragments' of HRM can be found. Storey (1992) finds that it is not an uncommon occurrence for HRM to be

Table 3.1 Hotel chains within the sample

Name	Frequency
Forte:	
Posthouse	14
Crest	10
Grand	6
Hotels	6
Heritage	2
Queen's Moat Hotels	18
Swallow Hotels	18
Thistle:	
Hotels	12
Mount Charlotte Thistle	2
Best Western	10
De Vere Hotels	10
Hilton	10
Holiday Inn:	
Hotels	5
Holiday Inn Garden Court	3
Holiday Inn Crowne Plaza	2
Marriott:	
Hotels	6
Courtyard by Marriott	2
Consort:	
Hotels	4
Crown	2
Copthorne	6
Friendly	6
Country Club Hotel Group	4
Jarvis	4
Principal	4
HIL	3
Leading Hotels	3
Novotel	3
Shire Inns	3
Campanile	2
Intercontinental	2
Radisson Edwardian	2
Ramada International	2
Forestdale	1
Hotel Ibis	1
Minotels of Britain	1
Sarova	1
Total chain hotels	190
Non-chain hotels	42

introduced alongside traditional structures rather than replacing them. The debate over the extent to which HRM has been adopted within the UK is made all the more inconclusive given that so little is known about HRM within the services. By testing the extent of adoption of HRM in a service setting, the analysis conducted here contributes towards this debate.

The next section describes the two surveys to be used within the analysis in further detail.

The data

The 1995 Survey of Human Resource Management in the Hotel Industry

The 1995 Survey of Human Resource Management in the Hotel Industry has three main sections. The section that will be the focus of attention here examines the adoption of HRM practices relating to terms and conditions of employment, recruitment, training, job design, pay systems, quality issues, communication and pay systems.

A further section within the questionnaire focuses on factors that are likely to influence the approach taken to HRM. Thus, information is collected on national ownership, the influence of the parent company, the size and nature of the personnel function, technical and organisational change, competitive strategy, number of employees, the proportion of the workforce employed on a part-time basis and the proportion of the workforce who are union members. An analysis of the factors that might influence HRM policy choice within the industry is presented within the following chapter.

The final part of the questionnaire looks at outcome measures. These measures include HR outcomes (for example, commitment of lower grades of staff to the organisation, workforce flexibility), employee relations outcomes such as disputes and absenteeism, and performance outcomes relating to financial performance, quality and productivity. An analysis of these data will demonstrate whether hotels adopting a more sophisticated approach towards their HRM practices report benefits in terms of superior effectiveness. This issue is addressed in Chapter 6.

Sample selection

Using the 1995 Automobile Association's UK Hotels guide as a source, hotels were selected for the sample using a straightforward size criterion, namely that they had 65 bedrooms or more. This figure was selected following initial piloting work suggesting that hotels above this size threshold would be likely to have an interest in HRM. Following initial piloting work, questionnaires were mailed to 660 hotels. In the event, usable replies were received from 232, a response rate of 35.15 per cent. Some questionnaires were not used as the respondents replied with reference to the organisation as a whole rather than with reference to the specific hotel to which the questionnaire had been mailed.

Representativeness of the sample

Because of the not inconsiderable data contained within the Automobile Association (AA) guide, it is possible to assess how representative the 232 responses to the questionnaire are of the total sample of 660 hotels. Assuming the AA guide itself is representative, such an assessment will reveal whether or not the sample achieved here is representative of UK hotels with more than 65 rooms.

Firstly, looking at star ratings, Table 3.2 shows a remarkable similarity between those who replied and the sample as a whole. Looking at the percentage ratings given to establishments by AA inspectors, a similar picture emerges, with the percentage ratings of respondents averaging 64.66 compared with 64.03 for the sample as a whole. There is therefore no evidence of bias on these two issues – in other words, there is nothing to suggest that only the better run or the higher quality hotels replied to the survey.

The fact that few of the hotels within the survey have a one or two star rating is not indicative of bias. This survey looks at larger hotels, which simply as a result of their size, are able to provide a wider range of facilities, and hence are likely to receive a higher star rating. Looking at the regional represen-

Table 3.2 Star ratings of respondents' hotels compared with the sample as a whole

Star rating	Respondents n=232	Whole sample n=660
1 star	0 (0)	1 (0.15)
2 stars	5 (2.16)	31 (4.7)
3 stars	95 (40.95)	312 (47.27)
4 stars	77 (33.29)	165 (25)
5 stars	11 (4.74)	27 (4.09)
Hotel groups (no rating given)	44 (18.97)	123 (18.64)
Town house classification	0 (0)	1 (0.15)

Note: Frequencies given. Percentages in brackets.

Table 3.3 Regional distribution of the respondents' hotels compared with the sample as a whole

Region	Respondents $n=232$	Whole sample $n=660$
London	29 (12.5)	94 (14.24)
South East	30 (12.93)	95 (14.39)
South West	26 (11.21)	90 (13.64)
East	22 (9.48)	58 (8.79)
East Midlands	16 (6.9)	33 (5)
West Midlands	21 (9.05)	57 (8.64)
North East	28 (12.07)	67 (10.15)
North West	29 (12.5)	75 (11.36)
Scotland	23 (9.91)	64 (9.7)
Wales	8 (3.45)	27 (4.09)

Note: Frequencies given. Percentages in brackets.

tativeness of the survey, as demonstrated by Table 3.3, there is also no particular evidence of systematic bias.

In the event, there was evidence of bias on two issues. Firstly, the price per room amongst the respondents was marginally higher at £89.61 compared with £84.79 for the sample as a whole. Secondly, concerning establishment size, there was some evidence to suggest that respondents within larger hotels were more inclined to reply. The average number of rooms among the respondents was 155.6, compared with 141.2 for the sample as a whole. The greater willingness of larger hotels to respond hints at the fact that interest in HRM may be positively correlated with establishment size. This issue is tested formally within the following chapter.

With the exception of these two issues, the evidence suggests that the 232 replies to the survey constitute a representative sample of the 660 hotels to which questionnaires were originally mailed.

The 1993 Survey of Human Resource Management in Greenfield Sites

The 1993 Survey of Human Resource Management in Greenfield Sites contains within it 322 manufacturing industry establishments (see Guest and Hoque (1994c) for a full description of the survey). Given that the establishments within this survey were asked the same questions about their HRM policies and practices as were the hotels within the 1995 Survey of Human Resource

Management in the Hotel Industry, this sample provides a control group against which the hotel industry establishments can be directly compared.

The response rate to the 1993 questionnaire was 38.5 per cent. This was achieved following reminders and a number of telephone calls, prior to which the response rate was 19 per cent. By contrast, the response rate of 35.15 per cent for the 1995 hotel industry survey was achieved without such reminders or telephone calls. This is in itself a revealing finding. Although there were differences between the 1993 and the 1995 surveys in terms of construction (the 1993 survey contained an additional section asking about HR policies and practices one year after start-up), and in the manner in which the data were collected (the 1995 survey was mailed to named individuals whereas the 1993 survey was addressed to 'The Personnel Manager'), there is still a remarkable difference in the initial response rates. This could be seen as indicative of the comparative levels of interest in issues relating to HRM between the two industries. At the very least, it calls into question the argument put forward by Price (1994), that it would be nonsensical to conduct research focusing on HRM within the hotel industry, as the industry is too far removed from the HRM ideal-type.

However, in utilising the two datasets discussed here for comparative purposes, a few potential caveats must be taken into account. Firstly, the 1993 survey was designed primarily to look at whether or not the HRM practices of greenfield-site establishments are any more sophisticated than are the HRM practices adopted within older establishments. As a result, the 1993 survey contains within it a disproportionate number of new and greenfield-site establishments. As the analysis of the survey revealed, greenfield-site establishments have indeed adopted a more sophisticated approach to HRM than have their older counterparts (Guest and Hoque, 1994c). The reported usage of HRM may therefore be higher amongst the establishments within the 1993 sample than across manufacturing industry as a whole.

Secondly, it must be considered whether or not the two samples to be used here are comparable from the point of view of establishment size. Looking at the 1995 hotel industry survey, the average number of employees per hotel is 125.42, and in the manufacturing survey the average number of employees is 235.59. If there is a relationship between establishment size and the likelihood of HRM being adopted, the fact that the manufacturing establishments within the sample are approximately twice as large as the hotels may introduce a bias into the results. However, if it is the case that all the establishments within the sample are over a size threshold above which HRM becomes relevant, this may not present a problem.

Thirdly, the two surveys under consideration were undertaken at separate points in time, with the manufacturing survey being undertaken two years prior to the hotel industry survey. Ideally, for comparative purposes, it would be preferable to have data on manufacturing and hotels at a single point in time, as a degree of change may have occurred within the manufacturing industry sample in the two-year interval between the timing of the two surveys. There is therefore the possibility that the reported usage of HRM may be slightly lower within the manufacturing sample than it would have been had the survey been conducted two years later at the time the hotel industry survey was conducted.

Bearing these caveats in mind, the next section describes the methods to be utilised to address the hypotheses outlined above.

Method of analysis

Both the 1993 and 1995 surveys obtained detailed information on HRM policies and practices. Bi-variate chi-square tests are used to ascertain whether any of the HRM techniques asked about are more widely reported in one industry than in the other.

Establishments with fewer than 25 employees, within which formal HRM procedures are unlikely to have much of a role to play, are dropped from the analysis. This results in eight manufacturing industry establishments being dropped from the analysis, yielding a subsample size of 314, and two hotels being dropped, yielding a subsample size of 230.

HRM practices

Concerning the specific HRM practices pursued, both surveys asked for information about terms and conditions of employment, recruitment and selection, training, job design, quality management, communication, consultation and pay systems. This list of practices is in part derived from Wood and Albanese (1995) and from Guest and Hoque (1994c). Table 3.4 contains a full listing of the questions asked in each of these areas.

HRM strategy

The data collected within the surveys enable a comparison of issues relating to HRM strategy and the extent to which HR issues are accorded strategic importance within both hotels and manufacturing.

Table 3.4 Usage of HRM practices in hotels and manufacturing

HRM practice	Hotels n=230 %	valid cases	Manuf. n=314 %	valid cases	Chi²
Terms and conditions					
Harmonised terms and conditions between management and non-management staff	76.11	226	65.5	313	.008
Single status for all staff	57.48	214	45.57	305	.008
Internal promotion the norm for appointments above the basic levels	90	230	81.79	313	.008
No compulsory redundancy	41.52	224	30.55	311	.009
Recruitment and selection					
Trainability as a major selection criteria	89.33	225	70.1	311	.000
Use of psychological tests as the norm for the selection of all staff	6.96	230	15.02	313	.004
Deliberate use of realistic job previews during recruitment and selection	54.46	224	51.66	302	.523
A formal system for communicating the values and systems in the company to new staff	87.33	230	71.57	313	.000
Training					
Deliberate development of a learning organisation	70	220	56.91	311	.002
An explicit policy requiring all staff to spend a specified minimum period annually in formal training	38.16	228	9.58	313	.000
Job design					
Flexible job descriptions that are not linked to one specific task	77.63	228	78.71	310	.765
Deliberate design of jobs to make full use of workers' skills and abilities (i.e. use of job enrichment and/or autonomous work groups)	56.39	227	52.44	307	.366
Work organised around teamworking for the majority of staff	79.39	228	69.58	309	.011
Staff involvement in setting performance targets	51.53	229	50.64	312	.838
Quality issues					
Production/service staff responsible for their own quality	65.79	228	86.22	312	.000
A majority of workers currently involved in quality circles or quality improvement teams	29.78	225	46.01	313	.000
Communication and consultation					
Regular use of attitude surveys to obtain the views of staff	50.88	228	21.73	313	.000
A system of regular, planned team briefing or cascade of information from senior management to the lower grades/shopfloor during which work stops	80.79	229	60.51	314	.000
All staff are informed about the market position, competitive pressures and establishment and company performance as a matter of course.	80.43	230	77.64	313	.43
Pay systems					
A merit element in the pay of staff at all levels	42.36	229	51.45	311	.037
Formal appraisal of all staff on a regular basis at least annually	89.08	229	61.66	313	.000

The first issue here relates to the strategic integration of HR decision-making with business strategy. As emphasised within the models presented by Schuler and Jackson (1987), Kochan and Barocci (1985) and Tichy *et al.* (1982) as well as the models presented by Guest (1987), Beer *et al.* (1985) and Walton (1985), the approach that is taken to HRM should be consciously tailored to meet the needs of the individual business. To assess the extent to which respondents view this as important, a question is asked as to whether an attempt has been made to deliberately integrate HR strategy with business strategy.

The second issue relating to strategic integration concerns internal fit. Irrespective of the individual HRM practices adopted, it is stressed universally within the HRM literature that those practices should cohere with each other and form part of an integrated, mutually supporting package rather than being seen as systems operating in isolation from each other. This is emphasised within Guest's (1987) goal of strategic integration, and also within Beer *et al.*'s (1985: 18) reference to the importance of fit between HRM policies and systems. In addition, there is increasing evidence that establishments introducing their HRM practices as a coherent package or bundle will outperform establishments within which HRM practices are introduced in an ad-hoc manner (see for example Ichniowski, Shaw and Prennushi, 1994; MacDuffie, 1995). In order to ascertain the extent to which such bundling is seen as important, respondents are asked whether their HRM practices are deliberately integrated with each other.

Thirdly, a series of questions is asked that attempts to ascertain the strategic importance accorded to HR issues. Respondents are asked firstly whether there is an HR strategy, formally endorsed and actively supported by senior management at the establishment. This will be indicative of the level within the organisational hierarchy at which HRM decision-making takes place. Secondly, the seriousness with which HR issues are taken from a strategic point of view is also likely to be reflected within the content of mission statements. As such, respondents are asked whether their establishment has a mission statement, and if so, whether it explicitly refers to HR issues.

The personnel function

Concerning the extent of development of the personnel function, only the hotel industry survey asked detailed questions concerning qualifications and staffing levels within the personnel department. However, as respondents were asked to state their job titles within both surveys, it is possible to assess whether the proportion of personnel specialists within the hotel industry sample varies significantly from the proportion of personnel specialists within the manufacturing industry sample.

As there are no further data within the 1993 manufacturing survey, a sub-sample of 315 manufacturing establishments that have a personnel specialist is taken from the third Workplace Industrial Relations Survey (WIRS3) in order to examine a wider range of personnel department features from a comparative perspective. However, several problems emerge when using WIRS3 for comparative purposes here. Firstly, the response rate to WIRS3 was 83 per cent, compared with 35.15 per cent within the 1995 hotel industry survey. Non-response bias therefore presents a potential problem. Secondly, WIRS3 was conducted in 1990. With the hotel industry survey being conducted five years later, it is possible that change over time will explain differences in the results achieved between the two samples. However, from the point of view of establishment size, the WIRS3 manufacturing subsample is still comparable with the hotel industry sample. Within WIRS3, the average number of employees within the manufacturing sector is 124.95 when the data are weighted to account for the fact that WIRS3 oversamples larger establishments, compared with 125.42 within the 1995 hotel industry sample.

While bearing the caveats discussed above in mind, it will be possible to use WIRS3 to look at issues concerning the relative levels of resourcing within personnel departments in relation to the time the respondent spends working on personnel issues, their qualifications and whether they have any support staff.

Results

Usage of HRM practices

What becomes immediately apparent from Table 3.4 is that there is no evidence whatsoever to suggest the reported usage of practices associated with an HRM approach is any lower within the hotel industry sample than within the manufacturing sample. In three of the areas examined, namely terms and conditions of employment, training and communication and consultation, the practices asked about are in fact more widely reported within the hotel industry sample than within the manufacturing sample.

Concerning the other policy areas, namely recruitment and selection, job design, quality issues and pay systems, the picture is less clear-cut. Nevertheless the results still by no means lend support to the thesis that hotels, at least those of the larger variety under investigation here, lag behind manufacturing establishments in terms of the reported adoption of HRM.

Firstly, looking at recruitment and selection, trainability is more frequently cited as a major selection criteria in the hotel industry, and formal systems for communicating the values and systems in the company to new staff are also more in evidence in hotels. However, the usage of realistic job previews is no higher, and the use of psychological tests as the norm for selection of all staff is lower amongst hotels. Indeed, only 6.9 per cent of the hotel industry sample claim to use psychological testing compared with 14.69 per cent of the manufacturing industry sample. Nevertheless, with the exception of this last issue, the hotel industry establishments seem to be just as careful as the manufacturing establishments in relation to the manner in which they recruit their staff.

Concerning job design, a higher proportion of respondents within the hotel industry sample claim to have adopted teamworking arrangements. On the other measures, however, namely flexible job descriptions not linked to one specific task and the deliberate design of jobs to make full use of workers' skills and abilities, there are no differences between hotels and manufacturing.

Looking at pay systems, fewer of the hotels use merit pay than do the manufacturing establishments, though hotels are more likely to carry out regular formal appraisals. Although performance appraisals in the hotel industry sample are used in all but seven cases where merit pay is used, it is nevertheless the case that 55.67 per cent of hotels adopting performance appraisals do not use them in conjunction with merit pay. Formal appraisals can serve either as an evaluative mechanism to determine merit pay awards, or they can serve a developmental or communicative purpose. The suggestion here is that in the hotel industry, they more commonly serve the latter of these purposes.

In one policy area, that of quality, the practices in question are less in evidence in hotels than in manufacturing. Firstly, employees in hotels are less likely to be responsible for their own quality. This is a surprise, as it might be expected that employees in the hotel industry would be accorded greater responsibility for service quality, given the difficulties involved within the hotel industry in terms of monitoring and controlling quality. If, on the other hand, service quality is considered to be of such importance within the overall product, it may be seen as too critical an issue to be left to individual employees. Hence, management might wish to maintain responsibility for quality via 'mystery customer' monitoring systems or 'brand standards' quality targets for example.

However, it is also surprising that fewer of the hotels claim to have set up quality improvement teams than have manufacturing establishments. Hotel employees experience hundreds of interactions with customers every day within their jobs. As Nightingale (1985) argues, staff knowledge of customer perceptions is potentially invaluable within continuous quality improvement processes, and management should ensure that such knowledge is tapped and utilised productively. The results here suggest that this is not happening within hotels to the extent to which it is happening in manufacturing.

Despite this latter result, the overall level of adoption of practices associated with an HRM approach is remarkably high within the hotel industry sample in comparison with the manufacturing sample. There is no evidence to suggest that the hotel industry lags behind manufacturing in terms of the adoption of new HRM practices. An analysis of this nature inevitably does not provide a comprehensive picture concerning the nature of HRM. Several unanswered questions remain, particularly in relation to the specific manner in which HRM practices operate and the spirit in which they were introduced. Nevertheless, the results here demonstrate a widespread willingness to adopt the rhetoric and discourse of HRM within the hotel industry. Whether there is substance behind this rhetoric is discussed within Chapter 5.

The existence of a formal HRM strategy

As can be seen from Table 3.5, the results would seemingly indicate that the hotels within the analysis approach the management of human resources in a more strategic manner than do their manufacturing industry counterparts.

Firstly, respondents within the hotel industry sample are more likely to report the existence of an HR strategy, formally endorsed and actively supported by senior management at the site, suggesting that responsibility for HR policy-making is located higher up the establishment hierarchy in hotels. The importance accorded to HR issues is further reflected by the fact that the hotels are more likely to have a mission statement, and mission statements within the hotel industry sample are just as likely to refer to HR issues as are mission statements within the manufacturing sample.

Moreover, a higher proportion of the respondents within the hotel industry sample claim to have achieved an integration between their HR policy and their business strategy. Similarly, the hotels are also more likely to claim to have deliberately integrated their practices with each other, possibly as part of an overall synergistic, mutually supporting configuration. Looking at Table 3.5, over 74 per cent of hotels claim to have deliberately integrated their HR practices with each other, compared with 54 per cent of establishments within the manufacturing sample.

Table 3.5 Comparison of HRM strategy in hotels and manufacturing

HRM policy	Hotels n=230		Manufacturing n=314		Chi2
	%	valid cases	%	valid cases	
HR strategy, formally endorsed and actively supported by top management	76.65	227	52.1	309	.000
HR policy deliberately integrated with business strategy	77.23	224	57.1	303	.000
Formal mission statement	84.72	229	56.61	295	.000
If there is a mission statement, does it explicitly refer to HR issues?	75.27	186	68.07	166	.134
HR practices deliberately integrated with each other	74.21	221	54	300	.000

Overall, the results in this section could be interpreted as indicative of a high level of acknowledgement within the hotel industry of the potential contribution which human resources, and the way in which they are managed, can make to the achievement of the goals of the business.

The results so far strongly endorse the positive conclusions reached within the more recent research conducted by Anastassova and Purcell (1995), Buick and Muthu (1997), Gilbert and Guerrier (1997), Harrington and Akehurst (1996) and Watson and D'Annunzio-Green (1996) in relation to the extent to which there has been experimentation with HRM within the industry. The evidence would seem to conflict with Lucas's claims that '… a strategic approach to managing employee relations expressed through an HRM strategy, is unlikely to be a prominent feature' (Lucas, 1995: 28).

Extent of development of the personnel function

Of the 225 hotel industry respondents who gave a job title, 138 (60 per cent) had 'personnel', 'human resources', 'employee resourcing' or 'training' within their job title. Looking at the manufacturing sample, the corresponding figure for the 307 respondents was 155 or 50.49 per cent.[2] Supporting Lucas's (1995, 1996) analysis of data from WIRS3, the figures suggest that there is proportionately a higher number of personnel specialists within the hotel industry sample than within the manufacturing sample.

As explained earlier, no further data were collected in relation to personnel departments within the 1993 manufacturing survey. Therefore, a subsample of 315 manufacturing firms that have a manager with responsibility for personnel issues is taken from WIRS3 in order to enable an examination of a wider range of personnel issues from a comparative perspective. These establishments are compared against the 132 hotels within the 1995 hotel industry survey that have a personnel specialist.

Firstly, looking at formal qualifications, 78.99 per cent of the hotel industry personnel specialists hold a qualification of some sort, ranging from City and Guilds to MBAs. As can be seen within Table 3.6, 47.83 per cent hold a specialist personnel management qualification (an IPD qualification, a degree in personnel management or a diploma in personnel management). This compares with a figure of 42.39 per cent within the WIRS3 manufacturing subsample. Specialists within the hotel industry subsample spend on average 70.54 per cent of their time working on personnel-related matters, in comparison with WIRS3 manufacturing respondents who spend 68.58 per cent of their time working on personnel-related matters. 85.83 per cent of the hotel industry respondents spend 50 per cent or more of their time working on personnel-related matters, compared with 77.08 per cent of the specialists within the WIRS3 manufacturing subsample. Finally, 59.42 per cent of hotels have staff other than the most senior manager responsible for personnel working specifically on personnel issues, compared with 42.2 per cent within the WIRS3 manufacturing subsample. Where support staff are in evidence within the hotel industry subsample however, their numbers are low, with there being only 1.8 support staff per department on average where any such staff were present.

Table 3.6 The personnel function within the hotel industry compared with the rest of the private sector

Personnel function	Hotels n=138		WIRS3 n=315	Manufacturing (79 when weighted)
	%	valid cases	%	valid cases (weighted)
Average percentage of time spent on personnel matters	70.54	127	68.58	71
Respondent spends ≥50% time on personnel matters	85.83	127	77.08	71
Respondent has formal qualification	47.83	138	42.39	79
Support staff present	59.42	138	42.2	78

Note: Data from WIRS3 are weighted. Percentages given.

As highlighted earlier, these results may be biased by the fact that WIRS3 was conducted five years prior to the hotel industry survey, hence the situation may have changed within manufacturing. Also, the response rate to WIRS3 is higher than the response rate to the hotel industry survey, so non-response bias may present a problem. Nevertheless, the results within Table 3.6 would seem to indicate that personnel specialists within the hotel industry are as well qualified as their manufacturing industry counterparts and are, if anything, more likely to be supported by back-up staff. The results presented here therefore support the conclusions reached by Kelliher and Johnson (1987, 1997), Lucas (1995, 1996) and Price (1994) concerning the increasing proportion of hotel industry establishments that have a specialist personnel manager, and the sophistication of those specialists in terms of their formal qualifications.

Discussion and conclusions

The findings reported within this chapter lend support to the currently emerging view that, at least within the larger hotels of the type examined within this analysis, there is nowadays a growing level of interest in HRM. The results also suggest that hotels of the type under investigation here attach a high degree of strategic importance to HR issues. There is no evidence whatsoever to suggest that manufacturing establishments demonstrate a greater interest in HRM than do comparatively sized hotels. If anything, the opposite is true.

This chapter also reports findings to support the currently emerging view that the occurrence of specialist personnel managers within the industry is more widespread than previously acknowledged (Lucas, 1995, 1996; Price, 1994). This does not necessarily suggest that the personnel specialists within the industry are playing an increasingly strategic role in terms of championing the adoption of more sophisticated HR practices. As argued by Lucas (1995, 1996) and Price (1994), the existence of personnel specialists may have more to do with the need for continual recruitment and basic skills training resulting from the industry's labour-intensive nature and high levels of labour turnover. This issue is tested empirically in the next chapter. The results here simply relate to the extent to which personnel managers are in existence within the industry, rather than the functions they perform.

It is important to reiterate that the hotels under investigation within this analysis are large by industry standards. This is deliberate, as it is only amongst these hotels that an interest in HRM might be expected. However, the conclusions reached here should not be extrapolated to smaller hotels, within which poor personnel practice, as described by Price (1994) for example, may well be commonplace. Nevertheless, as this analysis demonstrates, larger hotels would appear to have taken on board the need to improve and develop HR policy and practice. These hotels, by nature of their size and prominence may influence standards in the industry more widely.

It is also important to reiterate the caveat discussed earlier in relation to the timing of the two surveys used within this analysis. Ideally, it would be preferable to have data on the hotel industry and on manufacturing at the same point in time. The fact that the survey from which the manufacturing data were drawn was conducted two years prior to the hotel industry survey may have introduced a bias into the results.

Nevertheless, the results reported within this analysis would seem to corroborate the conclusions reached by Buick and Muthu (1997), Gilbert and Guerrier (1997) and Watson and D'Annunzio-Green (1996), concerning the extent to which the hotel industry has undergone change in recent years. It seems that as managers have taken on board the importance of service quality, they have also taken on board the need to find new ways of employing their staff. Much of the evidence portraying the hotel industry as backward and unstrategic dates back to the 1980s. Such conventional stereotypes now seem somewhat dated, at least where larger hotel establishments are concerned.

Finally, the findings reported within this chapter should be of interest not only to those whose primary research focus is within the hotel industry, but also to those with a broader interest in HRM. As discussed in the opening chapter, HRM as a concept is rooted firmly within a manufacturing paradigm, and its credibility will be seriously undermined if it is shown to be irrelevant or inapplicable within the services, within which almost 76 per cent of the working population is employed. However, the analysis here suggests a widespread adoption and considerable experimentation with new HRM initiatives within a service sector context, at least in terms of the adoption of the language and discourse of HRM. The extent to which there is substance behind this discourse will be considered in Chapter 5.

Notes

1   The results reported within this chapter are also reported in the *Human Resource Management Journal* 1999, 9(2).

2   Both of these figures omit those respondents who described themselves as regional personnel managers or directors, as this was taken as indicative that the personnel function was based at regional rather than unit level.

4   Influences on HRM in the hotel industry

The results presented within the previous chapter suggest that there has been a greater degree of experimentation with HRM within the hotel industry than has typically been given credit for in the past. The aim of this chapter is to assess the impact of factors that are likely to influence the approach taken to HRM within the industry.

As discussed within Chapters 1 and 2, several potential influences on HRM policy choice are considered to be important within both the mainstream HRM literature and the hotel industry literature. To recap briefly, these influences can be split into three categories. The first category concerns influences that are common to both sets of literature. These include the following:

i) Whether the hotel's business strategy emphasises tight cost control and competition on price factors, rather than service quality.

ii) The seriousness with which senior managers within the industry take HR issues, and more specifically whether personnel managers lack strategic vision and resources.

iii) Workforce characteristics, relating in particular to the extent to which the workforce is likely to prove resistant to the introduction of new style working practices. Related to this is the issue of establishment age. Within older establishments it might be expected that practices will be more entrenched in custom and practice, making the introduction of new approaches more difficult.

iv) Establishment size. HRM could be of limited relevance in the industry due to the smaller than average size of units. Conversely, HRM may be more applicable in hotels that are part of a chain.

v) The non-union nature of the industry. This could aid the introduction of an HRM approach, as it would not be necessary to gain trade union acquiescence prior to the introduction of new practices. However, if management choose to use their prerogative to introduce cost-cutting or labour-intensifying practices, it could also hinder the introduction of HRM.

vi) National ownership. Foreign owned hotels might operate a more sophisticated approach to HRM than their UK-owned counterparts.

The second category comprises influences on HRM that are seen as unique to the hotel industry. These include:

i)   The variable, just-in-time nature of demand within the industry. This may result in an emphasis on the use of peripheral or casual labour and numerical flexibility rather than on HRM.

ii) High levels of labour turnover. These may militate against the introduction of HRM as workforce instability hinders the development of shared values and the development of workforce competencies.

Given that these factors are seen as potentially highly influential within the hotel industry, the extent to which they influence decision-making will be critical in determining the extent to which the industry can genuinely be viewed as 'different'.

The third category concerns influences discussed exclusively within the HRM literature. Only one factor – the impact of financial markets – falls into this category. Establishments that are part of a diversified business may be less likely to have adopted HRM, as such an approach will conflict with the short-term profit maximising focus that is likely to emerge at head office level. While there is no corresponding discussion within the hotel industry literature on this issue, it would be sensible to hypothesise that where hotels are part of a diversified business, they will be subjected to the type of pressures as discussed within the mainstream HRM literature.

As can be seen from this categorisation, the majority of influences on HRM policy-making viewed as important within the hotel industry are common to both sets of literature. Indeed, the similarities between the influences on HRM discussed within the hotel industry and the mainstream literature resulted in the conclusion within Chapter 2 that there are few grounds, at least on the basis of a literature review, to argue that the hotel industry is really in any way 'different'.

The aim of this chapter is to test this assertion empirically by identifying the factors that exert the greatest influence on HRM policy choice. If the factors considered important within both sets of literature have the more substantial impact, this will add weight to the conclusion reached in Chapter 2, that the influences on management decision-making within the hotel industry are no different from the influences on management decision-making elsewhere. However, if the factors considered unique to the hotel industry have the larger impact, this will provide support for the argument that the industry is 'different', the implication being that managers in the industry do indeed face certain industry-specific contingencies.

Before looking at the methods and independent variables to be used to test the potential influences on HRM, the next section looks in detail at the dependent variable used to define HRM.

Defining human resource management

There is general agreement that HRM practices should be introduced as a mutually reinforcing, coherent package. This is stressed within Guest's (1987) goal of strategic integration, and also by Beer *et al.*'s (1985: 18) reference to the importance of fit between HRM practices and systems. Within the literature on performance, the degree of fit between practices is viewed as a key moderating factor (Huselid, 1995; MacDuffie, 1996).

However, there is a considerable lack of consensus over the specific practices that should be included within the HRM package. In their review of the more prominent models of HRM, Wood and Albanese (1995: 222–4) highlight several differences of opinion. For example, while Guest (1987) and Walton (1985) emphasise the provision of challenging jobs that eliminate the worst aspects of routinised work, this issue is by no means considered important by all the writers. Walton (1985) and Kochan and Dyer (1992) both put more emphasis on employment security than do UK-based theorists, although in operationalising HRM, the UK position on this issue is more closely mirrored by the recent empirical work by US management scholars Arthur (1994: 673) and Huselid (1995: 638). Wood and Albanese (1995) also draw attention to the disagreement over payment systems. For example, Purcell (1991: 40) considers merit pay or performance-related pay to be an essential part of the commitment building process. However, Beer *et al.* (1984: 147) state that the focus within commitment-enhancing HRM should be on non-wage factors and not on pay-for-performance systems that emphasise the cash-nexus nature of the employment relationship. Variation in the design of HRM practices is also demonstrated within comparisons of organisations of different national origins. For example, Guest and Hoque (1996) find support for the hypothesis that US-owned companies will emphasise unitarist, individualistic practices and Japanese companies will emphasise single status, job security and team-working. Given the not inconsiderable differences between the more prominent theoretical models of HRM, Guest (1997) suggests that just about the only common emphasis within the models is the importance attached to training.

Thus, whereas there is a general agreement that HRM practices should be introduced within a mutually reinforcing package, there is greater debate over the specific practices that should be included within that package. It seems that there is no necessary 'one best way' theoretical model to achieve desired HR outcomes, but 'several best ways'. Some might emphasise training, others might emphasise employee involvement and others might emphasise job design. No one approach is necessarily superior to another. As such, HRM is perhaps better viewed as a philosophy of management, rather than as a specific set of practices or tools, which management can introduce to achieve desired HR outcomes.

However, if HRM is to be viewed as a philosophy of management rather than as a set of prescribed techniques, its operationalisation becomes somewhat difficult given the equifinite configurations of practices that can be adopted. Several approaches to the construction of a dependent HRM variable have been taken in the past, for example, within one part of his analysis, Huselid (1995) takes a straightforward cumulative count of the number of HR practices used. While dealing with the need for equifinality, such an approach misses the critical issue that practices should cohere each other. By ignoring this issue, such an approach is unable to distinguish between those firms that have introduced HRM in a piecemeal, cherry-picked manner, and those that have introduced a coherent set of policies, deliberately and consciously designed to synergistically support each other.

Wood (1996) and Wood and Albanese (1995) take an alternative approach. Their 'latent variable' analysis examines the manner in which HRM practices cluster together. They then look at each cluster, and determine which cluster most accurately resembles a theoretical model of 'high commitment manage-ment'. However, given that the theoretical position itself is ambiguous, such an approach leaves much to the researchers discretion as to which clusters are representative of 'high commitment management' and those which are not. As stressed within the theoretical discussions, different firms in different situations may accentuate differing practices within their HRM policy. It is therefore difficult to see how this approach, which relies on a pre-determination on the part of the researcher as to which particular cluster should be defined as HRM, can deal with the equifinite approaches to HRM that may exist in practice.

The dependent variable to be used here therefore attempts to address both the need for equifinality and also the need for a coherent, strategically integrated approach. The variable is dichotomous, hence it identifies hotels that can be considered to be practising some sort of coherent approach to HRM, and those that are not. To be categorised as a user of HRM, the hotel must be using above the mean number of HR practices asked about (in this case at least 14 out of 22 – see Chapter 4 for a detailed description of these practices), and must also have provided a positive response to the question asking whether HR practices are deliberately integrated with each other.

This approach overcomes the problems highlighted above in two ways. Firstly, it is highly likely that hotels practising some form of HRM, whatever the precise configuration, are using a wide range of HR practices. They may all be attempting to practise an HRM approach, but in doing so may emphasise different HRM practices. Thus, hotels likely to have adopted some form of HRM approach can be identified, without the imposition of any arbitrary pre-determined definition as to what that approach should consist of. As such, the variable is able to take into account the need for equifinality.

Secondly, the variable overcomes the problems encountered when using a measure based on a cumulative count of the number of practices adopted. A cumulative count fails to distinguish establishments that have introduced their HRM practices in a piecemeal manner from those that have introduced them as part of a coherent package. Requiring 'HRM' hotels to have made an attempt to strategically integrate their HR practices with each other addresses this problem.

Based on the definition described above, there are 73 (46.5 per cent) hotels that are defined as having adopted an HRM approach and 84 (53.5 per cent) that have not.

Independent variables and method of analysis

The data used here are drawn from the 1995 Survey of Human Resource Management in the UK Hotel Industry, described in detail in the previous chapter. When missing data are accounted for, the sample size is 157. As discussed earlier, the aim of the analysis to be conducted here is to assess the impact of the range of potential influences on the adoption of an HRM approach. This section describes the variables to be used to test the impact of these influences. In doing so, the variables in question are divided into internal and external influences. This will enable conclusions to be drawn as to whether external environmental factors such as market contingencies play a more powerful role in shaping HR policy than do internal organisational factors such as establishment size or workforce characteristics.

Internal variables

Workforce resistance to change

According to Guest (1987), workforce resistance to change is an important factor in explaining why firms within the UK have failed to adopt HRM. In order to test the impact of workforce resistance to change on the extent to which HRM has been adopted in the hotel industry, respondents were asked firstly whether there has been an attempt to implement either a major technical change (e.g. introduction of computers or cooking/vending equipment), or a major organisational change (e.g. introduction of work teams, delayering or decentralisation of decision-making) in the last six years (or since operations commenced if the establishment is less than six years old).

If the reply to either of these two questions was positive, respondents were then asked the extent to which the workforce offered resistance to the most recent programme of change, on a scale of one to five, where one was 'very low', and five was 'very high'. A final question asked whether or not the resistance offered was sufficient to prevent the change from being implemented.

This series of questions assesses the impact of workforce resistance by firstly indicating whether resistance has proved sufficient to prevent the introduction of a proposed change. Secondly, the inclusion in the multivariate analysis of variables looking at the extent to which there has been resistance to change will show whether the introduction of HRM has been hampered in situations where the workforce has demonstrated a willingness or tendency to resist change.

Management innovation and strategy

The questions described above relating to resistance to change capture information on whether there have been attempts to introduce organisational and technical change within the last six years or since the hotel opened (if less than six years old). This information will enable an evaluation of the impact of management willingness to innovate. Guest (1987) and Sisson and Storey (1990) attach particular importance to this issue, arguing that the failure to adopt HRM is often the result of management inability to handle change effectively. The aim here, therefore, will be to test whether managers that have displayed an overall willingness to embrace change generally are more likely to have innovated in terms of HRM. Whether or not the 89 (56.7 per cent) hotels that have attempted technical change or the 98 (62.42 per cent) hotels that have attempted organisational change in the last six years are more likely to have adopted HRM will shed light on this issue.

Workplace age

On a new site, unrestricted by problems of resistance to change, entrenched attitudes and working practices, management have the opportunity to introduce the practices they would ideally like to use. This is tested empirically by Guest and Hoque (1993) who demonstrate that, using data from WIRS3, greenfield-site establishments have indeed adopted a more sophisticated approach to HRM. Similarly, within the hotel industry, Mars, Bryant and Mitchell (1979) found a hotel on a new site, employing 'green' labour which had no preconceived notions in relation to job design in the industry, to have successfully introduced multi-skilling with positive results.

It is not possible to identify greenfield sites as such within the hotel industry data used here. However, it will be possible to evaluate the relationship between establishment age and the likelihood of HRM being practised to assess whether or not newer hotels have been more successful in adopting the approach to HRM they would ideally like to see.

Peripheral employment

As a result of seasonal and daily variations in demand for the hotel industry product, an above average proportion of the industry workforce is employed on a part-time or temporary basis. A heavy focus on numerical flexibility and the usage of peripheral workers is likely to, according to Guerrier and Lockwood (1989b) and Walsh (1991), hinder the adoption of an HRM approach.

The inclusion of a variable looking at the proportion of part-time employees to total employees in the regression will demonstrate whether or not there is a negative association between the adoption of HRM and part-time working.[1]

. 23.97 per cent of the total number of employees within the subsample under investigation here are working on a part-time basis.

Trade unions

Within the HRM literature, there is considerable debate as to whether a trade union presence encourages or militates against the implementation of HRM (see Trades Union Congress (1994), Guest (1995), Guest and Dewe (1991), Beer *et al.* (1985), Beaumont (1992) for insights into this debate). If, as argued by Guerrier and Lockwood (1989a), managers within the hotel industry are pursuing a strategy based on cost reduction, it is possible that the autonomy resulting from non-unionism will facilitate the introduction of labour-intensifying or wage cost minimising practices, which would be resisted by trade unions if deemed exploitative. Conversely, the lack of trade unions may give managers the opportunity to experiment with HRM without having to firstly gain trade union acquiescence.

A variable is therefore included within the analysis that will evaluate the impact of a trade union presence within the industry. Within the sample, only 17 (10.83 per cent) hotels have a trade union presence, and average membership where a trade union is present is only 10.29 per cent. The intention was also to test whether unions have a stronger influence on the approach taken to HRM where they are recognised for pay-bargaining purposes. However, only five (3.18 per cent) hotels claim to actually recognise the union(s) that are present. As such it is not possible to test whether management behaviour would be moderated in the face of more powerful or well-organised trade unions, as there are too few recognised unions for a reliable estimate of their effect. The only test that can be carried out relates to the influence of the weak form of trade unionism that exists within the industry as delineated by trade union presence.

Labour turnover

It is usual to treat the level of labour turnover as a measure of the effectiveness of HRM. However, in the case of the hotel industry, it makes sense to treat turnover as an independent variable, as much of the debate concerns its likely impact on the introduction of HRM in the first instance. The hotel industry workforce is highly unstable, as demonstrated by a level of labour turnover well above the average for the economy as a whole. This may militate against the adoption of HRM in two ways. Firstly, the stability necessary for the successful introduction of shared values is lacking (Nailon, 1989). Secondly, Wood (1992: 22–3) claims that high labour turnover is endemic and institutionalised within the industry. As such, the introduction of HRM would do little or nothing to alleviate it, so it is unlikely that management would attempt such an approach. Moreover, it is not clear within the industry whether or not managers see labour turnover as a problem (Johnson, 1985), as they can use it to shed inefficient staff and to reduce headcount quickly and cheaply. Given the potential cost control benefits of high levels of labour turnover and the fact that an inherently unstable workforce is unlikely to respond to HRM, it seems sensible to hypothesise that the higher the level of labour turnover, the less likely it is that experimentation with HRM will have been attempted.

Average labour turnover for 1994 within the sample being looked at here was 34.17 per cent, with turnover within individual hotels ranging from 2 per cent to 95 per cent. To ascertain the relationship between the adoption of HRM and labour turnover, a series of dummy variables looking at hotels with 0–20 per cent, 21–40 per cent, 41–60 per cent and over 60 per cent labour turnover in 1994 will be included within the analysis.

Workplace size

Mullins (1993) makes the point that because of the importance of location, hotels cannot centralise the production of the service they supply. Hence, they tend to be small in size. Indeed, the Department of National Heritage estimates that 81 per cent of hotels have fewer than 25 employees (Department of National Heritage, 1996). In addition, hotels with more than 25 employees tend to be smaller than establishments in other industries. Within WIRS3, which samples establishments with 25 or more employees, the average number of employees within hotels is 62.25, compared with 91.92 for the rest of the private sector, when the data are weighted.

HRM may be of little relevance within smaller establishments where inter-personal contact between owners or managers and employees is greater and personal relationships or a family atmosphere are likely to negate the need for formal procedures. To test this issue, a series of dummy variables looking at hotels employing 25–49, 50–99, 100–199 and 200 or more staff is included within the analysis. It is worth reiterating that the sample used here is of hotels that are much larger than the industry average. If the relationship between size and HRM is weak, this may simply suggest that there is a particular establishment-size threshold within the industry above which HRM has a role to play. It will be important not to extrapolate the results to smaller hotels, on which such a finding would have no bearing.

National ownership

A body of literature has developed recently concerning the approach to HRM adopted within establishments of differing national origin. This includes the literature on Japanese transplants (for example, Oliver and Wilkinson, 1989, 1992; Trevor and White, 1983; Wickens, 1987; Wood, 1996) and the literature on German-owned companies (for example, Beaumont, Cressey and Jakobsen, 1990; Guest, 1996; Guest and Hoque, 1996). Lucas and Laycock (1991) and Price (1994) suggest that within the hotel industry, foreign-owned establishments have adopted a more sophisticated approach to HRM than have domestically owned establishments, and they will reap rewards in terms of financial performance and market share as a result. As such, this issue is particularly worthy of analysis.

Within the sample looked at here, 24 (15.29 per cent) hotels describe themselves as foreign owned. A variable will be included to ascertain whether these establishments are any more likely to have introduced an HRM approach than are domestically owned establishments.

Chain hotels

As discussed in Chapter 2, Shamir (1978) suggests that a more formal and sophisticated approach to HRM is likely to be found amongst hotels that are part of a chain. They are more likely to have a formal strategy dictated to them from above as the corporate centre will not only be concerned with the efficiency of individual business units, but they will also wish to achieve a consistency of approach in order that staff can be easily moved around within the organisation as a whole. By contrast, independently owned hotels are able to rely on an informal family atmosphere and interpersonal relationships between staff and owners, and they do not need to worry about the need for a formal, consistent approach between units.

To test whether or not such arguments hold true within these data, a variable is included that identifies chain hotels. 131 or 83.44 per cent of the hotels within the sample fit this description, though it must be remembered that the chains vary in size from the large chains such as Forte and Thistle to much smaller chains such as Sarova or Minotels of Britain (Table 3.1 in the previous chapter contains a complete list of the hotel chains within the sample). Nevertheless, this variable will demonstrate whether chain hotels are indeed more likely to have introduced an HRM approach, as hypothesised earlier.

Extent of development of the personnel department

The need for a well-developed personnel function if HRM is to flourish is emphasised within the mainstream HRM literature. Guest and Hoque (1994a) find that where an establishment has a well-developed personnel department, it is more likely to have adopted practices associated with an HRM approach. Similarly, within the hotel industry literature, Boella (1986:33) suggests that the future role of personnel managers could be to encourage a more participative approach to decision-making.

In order to test the impact of the unit-level personnel function on the approach taken to HRM in the hotel industry, a series of measures, the frequencies for which can be found in Chapter 4, have been developed. These are as follows:

a)   Whether or not there is a manager at the hotel with specific responsibility for personnel issues.
b)   If the answer to a) was positive:
  –   Whether or not the manager responsible for personnel spends 50 per cent or more of their time working on personnel issues.
  –   Whether or not the manager responsible for personnel has a formal qualification in personnel management or a related subject.
  –   The number of staff, with the exception of the most senior manager responsible for personnel, who work specifically within the personnel department of the hotel.

The inclusion of these variables within the multivariate analysis will demonstrate the impact of the nature and development of personnel departments on the approach taken to HRM within the industry.

The location of HR decision-making

The final issue to be tested in relation to factors internal to the organisation concerns Guest's (1987) argument that if HRM is to flourish, responsibility for HR decision-making should be fully integrated into the strategic planning process at senior management levels. To test this issue, a dichotomous variable has been constructed that asks whether or not the hotel has a human resource strategy that is formally endorsed and actively supported by senior management at the hotel. Within the sample used here 121 (77.07 per cent) hotels claim to have such a strategy. As stressed in the previous chapter, this is high in comparison with manufacturing. The aim here is to assess the impact of the location of decision-making in relation to HRM issues within hotels on the approach taken to HRM.

External variables

This section describes the variables to be used to test the impact of a range of potential influences relating to the environment within which hotels operate on the approach taken to HRM.

Product markets and competitive strategy

As argued within the situational contingency typology presented by Schuler (1989) and Schuler and Jackson (1987), an HRM approach will be considered more applicable in situations where product markets dictate quality enhancement to be the key to competitive advantage. Conversely, HRM will be considered inappropriate in instances where product markets emphasise cost control.

The Schuler (1989) and Schuler and Jackson (1987) hypothesis is tested as follows. Firstly, from a choice of price, quality, cost control, responsiveness to customer needs, advertising/marketing, providing a distinctive service or 'other replies', respondents are asked to state the two features that most accurately describe their hotel's approach to business strategy. A variable is then created that splits the sample into hotels emphasising a quality enhancer approach and hotels emphasising a cost reducer approach. A third category is added, comprising hotels with a somewhat more ambiguous approach to business strategy (possibly representing those establishments that Porter (1985) would describe as 'stuck in the middle').

Hotels specifying the following features of their service to be the most crucial for competitive success are designated as cost reducers:

- price AND one of the following:
- cost control
- OR responsiveness to customer needs
- OR advertising/marketing
- OR providing a distinctive service
- OR human resources (listed by respondent in the 'other replies' space.

Also included as cost reducers are those who state the following features are the most crucial to competitive success:

- cost control AND one of the following:
- responsiveness to customer needs
- OR advertising/marketing
- also 'responsiveness to customer needs' AND 'value for money' (listed by a respondent in the 'other replies' space).

Thirty-six (22.93 per cent) hotels within the sample fall into this category.

Hotels specifying the following are designated as quality enhancers:

- quality AND one of the following:
- responsiveness to customer needs
- OR advertising/marketing
- OR providing a distinctive service.

Seventy-three (46.5 per cent) hotels within the sample fall into this category.

Hotels specifying the following are designated as 'others':

- price and quality
- quality and cost control
- responsiveness to customer needs AND one of the following:
- advertising/marketing
- OR providing a distinctive service
- OR cleanliness
- OR workforce skills
- OR responsiveness to staff needs.

The latter three responses were given in the 'other replies' space by respondents. Forty-eight (30.57 per cent) hotels fall into this category.

The main aim of this categorisation is to assess whether hotels emphasising quality enhancement are more likely to have adopted HRM than have hotels emphasising cost reduction. However, the finding that 46.5 per cent of the sample view quality enhancement as the key feature of their business strategy compared with 22.93 per cent who view cost minimisation as the key, is in itself a noteworthy finding. Callan (1994), Kokko and Moilanen (1997), Mattsson (1994), Olsen (1989) and Pye (1994) argue that quality enhancement is becoming increasingly important for competitive success within the industry. The classification here demonstrates that a large proportion of hotels within this sample have apparently taken this message on board.

The AA hotels guide, on which the 1995 hotel industry survey was based, contains information on two further issues relating to strategy. The first concerns the star rating of the hotel, and the second concerns the price of a standard double room per night. HRM might be viewed as more relevant within four or five-star hotels or within more expensive hotels, given the greater emphasis on service quality that might be expected. Within the sample, 2 hotels are categorised as two-star, 72 are three-star, 50 are four-star, 6 are five-star and 27 are unclassified (company-owned chain hotels). The mean price of a double room per night within the subsample under investigation here is £87.40. There is considerable variation however, the cheapest price quoted within the sample being £39 per night, the most expensive being £264. Variables describing both the star rating of the hotel and also the price per night are included in the analysis. This will demonstrate whether it is only the higher star-rated hotels, or the more expensive hotels that have adopted HRM, or whether experimentation with HRM has occurred across all the star categories and across the whole price range.

Market stability

As seasonality is likely to result in the need for a large number of temporary or casual workers, it might be expected that where hotels operate within particularly seasonal markets there will be less scope for an HRM approach. To test this relationship, a three-part variable is used which asks whether the market for the hotel's services is stable, seasonal but predictable or unpredict-able. Eighty (50.96 per cent) hotels within the sample fall into the first category, 65 (41.4 per cent) fall into the second and 12 (7.64 per cent) fall into the third. This, in itself, is a revealing result. Over half of the hotels within the sample do not report any seasonal fluctuation in demand. This may be due to the fact that many of the hotels within the sample are large city-centre hotels with corporate clients comprising the major clientele, whose demand for hotel services is year-round (although business trade tends to dip in August, this is predictable, and can sometimes be compensated for by passing holiday trade). Therefore, although the usage of HRM may be lower amongst hotels experiencing seasonal fluctuations, it should be remembered that seasonality may not be a major logistical problem for the type of hotel under investigation within this sample.

Impact of decentralisation

To test the argument put forward by Kirkpatrick, Davies and Oliver (1992) and Purcell (1989), that HRM is less likely to have been adopted among establishments that have decentralised as a result of pressure from financial markets, the following series of questions were asked. Firstly, respondents were asked about the level of influence of their parent company – on a scale of one to five (where one is 'very low' and five is 'very high') – over the hotel's financial control (e.g. cost centres, profit centres, setting budgets and performance targets). They were then asked whether their parent company and its subsidiaries were best described as a single business (more than 90 per cent of sales in one line of business), a dominant business (70–90 per cent of sales in one line of business), a related business (no single line of business accounts for more than 70 per cent of sales but businesses are related to each other), or a conglomerate business (many unrelated businesses). If the theory is of explanatory value in the hotel industry, less evidence of HRM would be expected amongst hotels that are part of a related or conglomerate business, in particular where a high degree of financial control is exercised by the corporate centre (in other words, where the hotel fits the description of the type of business unit described by Kirkpatrick, Davies and Oliver (1992) and Purcell (1989)).

Two variables have been constructed to examine this issue. The first enables a comparison of the approaches taken to HRM in the 24 (17.02 per cent) hotels that are part of a conglomerate business, the 46 (32.62 per cent) that are part of a related business, the 33 (23.4 per cent) that are part of a dominant business and the 38 (26.95 per cent) that are part of a single business. It would be expected that interest in HRM would be lower in hotels that are part of a conglomerate business.

A second variable tests the theory more precisely. This variable looks at hotels that are part of a related or conglomerate business and whose parent has a fairly or very high level of influence over financial control. Fifty-one (36.17 per cent) hotels within the sample fit this description. If decentralisation impacts as predicted on HRM policy choice within the hotel industry, it would be expected that hotel units within such organisations would be less likely to have adopted HRM.

Further control variables

All regressions control for the region in which the hotel is located.

Results

The impact of internal factors

What becomes immediately apparent from equation 1 in Table 4.1 is that there is very little relationship between many of the internal factors and the likelihood of an HRM approach having been adopted. Firstly, the slight relationship with workforce size suggests that the medium-sized hotels within the sample (employing between 100 and 199 staff) have been marginally more successful in introducing HRM. Apart from this, the coefficients of the other size dummies suggest a general applicability of HRM within the size of hotels covered by this sample, with there being no evidence that the smaller hotels (employing between 25 and 49 staff) are less likely to have adopted an HRM approach than hotels employing more than 200 staff, for example. As stated earlier, given that the hotels being looked at here are much larger than the hotel industry average, it is important not to extrapolate this result to hotels with fewer than 25 employees.

Secondly, contrary to expectations, there is nothing to suggest that operating with a high proportion of part-time workers hinders the adoption of an HRM approach. It may be the case therefore that part-time workers should not necessarily be viewed as peripheral. Given the high proportion of female employees within the industry workforce, it may be the case that such working arrangements suit both workforce as well as management. Simply because these workers work fewer hours per week than do full-time staff, there is no reason why they should be any less committed, or indeed any less likely to respond favourably to HRM, particularly if they are working part-time out of choice. Alternatively, it may be the case that where there is a high proportion of part-time peripheral workers, HRM is applied exclusively to the core, full-time workforce.

The insignificant union presence variable suggests that the weak unionism within the industry neither encourages nor hinders management in implementing the policies of their choice. It is worth reiterating here, however, that nothing is known about whether a stronger form of unionism would have a more potent impact.

Looking at the establishment age dummies, there is nothing to support either the hypothesis that policies will mature or become more sophisticated over time, or the alternative hypothesis that new establishments are more likely to be have adopted an HRM approach, having been in a position to introduce from scratch the policies they would ideally like to use.

Table 4.1 Relationship between HRM and internal factors in the hotel industry

	Equation 1	*Equation 2*	*Equation 3*	*Equation 4*
Total employment:				
50–99	.555 (.702)	.564 (.71)	.735 (.757)	.556 (.751)
100–199	1.234 (.718)*	1.154 (.723)	1.267 (.765)*	1.22 (.761)
200+	.868 (.872)	.808 (.876)	.963 (.918)	.633 (.914)
Proportion of workforce				
part-time	−.394 (1.018)	−.072 (1.042)	−.044 (1.104)	.091 (1.104)
Union presence	−1.023 (.652)	−.692 (.691)	−.827 (.73)	−.978 (.73)
Part of a chain	1.295 (.564)**	.852 (.615)	1.071 (.646)*	.927 (.652)
Age:				
6–10 yrs	−.2 (.49)	−.193 (.501)	−.313 (.519)	−.248 (.524)
10–20 yrs	.607 (.57)	.689 (.585)	.453 (.606)	.611 (.604)
20 yrs +	.476 (.518)	.393 (.523)	.282 (.541)	.164 (.551)
Foreign owned	1.31 (.582)**	1.227 (.594)**	1.285 (.613)**	1.314 (.613)**
Personnel specialist	−.321 (.447)	−.252 (.455)	−.255 (.461)	−.123 (.474)
HR strategy		.99 (.518)*	.853 (.547)	.791 (.542)
Technical change:				
fairly low resistance			−.085 (.605)	
medium resistance			.352 (.723)	
fairly/very high resistance			−.349 (1.061)	
no change attempted			−.825 (.526)	
Organisational change:				
fairly low resistance				−.363 (.664)
medium resistance				−.012 (.685)
fairly/very high resistance				−.638 (.864)
no change attempted				−1.371 (.64)**
Pseudo R^2	.129	.147	.169	.187
n	157	157	157	157

Notes: Dependent variable 1 = HRM hotels, 0 = non-HRM hotels.
Logit analysis. Coefficients given (standard errors in brackets).
All regressions control for region.
* significant at 10 per cent, ** significant at 5 per cent.

Indeed, within the first equation, only two factors stand out as being associated with an HRM approach. Firstly, hotels that describe themselves as foreign owned have apparently adopted a more sophisticated approach. This is a robust result, which does not change when further controls are added either in Table 4.1, or later in Tables 4.2 and 4.3. The result here therefore supports the argument put forward by Lucas and Laycock (1991) and Price (1994), that foreign-owned hotels in the UK are likely to have adopted more sophisticated approaches to HRM than have UK-owned hotels.

Table 4.2 Resistance to organisational and technical change in the hotel industry

	Resistance to technical change	Resistance to organisational change
Very low	32 (35.96)	19 (19.39)
Fairly low	36 (40.45)	37 (37.76)
Medium	15 (16.85)	30 (30.61)
Fairly high	5 (5.62)	12 (12.24)
Very high	1 (1.12)	0
Total	89	98
Mean score	1.96	2.36

Note: Frequencies given. Percentages in brackets.

Secondly, there is some evidence to suggest that chain hotels are more likely to have adopted an HRM approach. This result is moderated by the inclusion of the HR strategy variable. The suggestion is therefore that chain hotels are more likely to have adopted an HRM approach because HR issues are taken more seriously by senior management within these hotels, as measured by the existence of an HR strategy, formally endorsed and actively supported by senior management. Indeed, only 42.31 per cent of hotels that are not part of a chain claim to have such a formal HR strategy, compared with 83.97 per cent of hotels that are part of a chain. However, the relationship between the seriousness with which HR issues are taken at senior management level and the adoption of an HRM approach is weak in equation 2 of Table 4.1 and disappears completely from equation 3 onwards. This suggests that there is no automatic relationship between the existence of a formally supported HR strategy and the adoption of an HRM approach *per se*. It may be the case that such a relationship only exists within chain hotels.

Equations 3 and 4 of Table 4.1 look at resistance to change issues. As demonstrated by Table 4.2, resistance to technical change is rather low. Resistance to organisational change is somewhat higher, with almost 43 per cent of hotels that have attempted a major organisational change in the last six years having reported medium or fairly high levels of resistance. This supports the conclusions reached by Daniel (1987), who finds that resistance to organisational change is higher than resistance to technical change as it is more likely to be associated with fear of job loss, and the conclusion reached by Handy (1985) who argues that 'role strain' may result from a fear of an expansion of job roles or an increase in responsibilities in the face of organisational change.

Concerning the impact of resistance to change, none of the technical change attempts had failed as a result of workforce resistance and only one of the hotels within the sample reported that the last organisational change attempt had failed as a result of such resistance. This suggests one of two things. Firstly, it might be the case that workforce resistance to change can be overcome quite easily, perhaps via a participative or a normative re-educative approach. Alternatively, it might be the case that change initiatives are pushed through irrespective of the views or fears of the workforce. Which of these two scenarios is closest to the truth can be addressed within the case study interviews. Nevertheless, the tendency of the workforce to resist does not seem to have exerted any influence on managerial policy choice in relation to HRM. Within equations 3 and 4 in Table 4.1, there is no suggestion of a relationship between the extent to which the workforce has demonstrated a tendency to resist change and the likelihood of an HRM approach being pursued.

It is further hypothesised above that where management has displayed innovative behaviour in relation to technical and organisational change, HRM is also more likely to have been adopted. Equations 1 and 2 in Table 4.3 show that where there has been both organisational and technical change in the last six years or since operations began, establishments are indeed more likely to be practising an HRM approach. Equation 3 in Table 4.3 would seem to indicate that major organisational change has been the more influential factor, with the significance of the major technical change variable disappearing with the intro- duction of the organisational change variable. The results therefore suggest a tendency for hotels to have adopted HRM hand-in-hand with an overall package of organisational change. This is further demonstrated by the fact that hotels that have attempted organisational change are also more likely to have an HR strategy, formally endorsed and actively supported by senior management. To be precise, 83.67 per cent of hotels that have experienced an organisational change attempt in the last six years have a formal HR strategy, compared with 66.1 per cent of those that have not, a result that is significant in a chi-square test.

This result has one further implication. The inclusion of a change variable into the equation introduces a notion of dynamics. In that it is quite strongly linked to organisational change having taken place within the last six years, innovation in terms of HRM itself within the industry may well be quite a recent phenomenon in many hotels.

Equation 1 of Table 4.4 sheds light on the relationship between HRM and the nature of the personnel department. Looking back firstly to equation 1 of Table 4.1, there is no relationship between the presence of a personnel specialist

Table 4.3 The relationship between HRM, technical and organisational change in the hotel industry

	Equation 1	Equation 2	Equation 3
Total employment:			
50–99	.723 (.742)	.645 (.749)	.712 (.761)
100–199	1.26 (.756)*	1.253 (.761)*	1.292 (.773)*
200+	.951 (.906)	.74 (.904)	.828 (.918)
Proportion part-time	−.047 (1.061)	.074 (1.087)	.062 (1.09)
Union presence	−.819 (.715)	−.993 (.722)	−1.026 (.734)
Part of a chain	1.133 (.635)*	.941 (.644)	1.081 (.655)*
Establishment age			
6–10 yrs	−.293 (.514)	−.275 (.523)	−.328 (.528)
11–20 yrs	.448 (.607)	.543 (.595)	.427 (.61)
20 yrs +	.274 (.53)	.203 (.541)	.17 (.544)
Foreign owned	1.268 (.605)**	1.326 (.61)**	1.343 (.615)**
Personnel specialist present	−.233 (.457)	−.163 (.487)	−.171 (.468)
HR strategy	.829 (.531)	.791 (.537)	.737 (.542)
Attempt to implement:			
major technical change	.834 (.404)**		.466 (.446)
major organisational change		1.153 (.422)**	.961 (.459)**
Pseudo R^2	.167	.182	.188
n	157	157	157

Notes: Dependent variable 1 = HRM hotels, 0 = non-HRM hotels.
Logit analysis. Coefficients given (standard errors in brackets).
All regressions control for region.
* significant at 10 per cent, ** significant at 5 per cent.

and the adoption of an HRM approach. Equation 1 of Table 4.4 looks in more detail at hotels where there is a personnel specialist. This equation shows that personnel specialists are no more likely to be responsible for introducing HRM irrespective of the qualifications they hold, the amount of time they spend working on personnel issues or the number of support staff they have working on personnel issues.

On the basis of the results presented here, it would seem that unit-level personnel is not responsible for the introduction of more sophisticated approaches to HRM. What, therefore, is their role? This is, at least in part, revealed by the fact that labour turnover in hotels where there is a personnel specialist present is on average 38.13 per cent, compared with only 28.71 per cent where there is no such specialist. Thus, one important task of the unit-

Table 4.4 The relationship between HRM, the personnel function and labour turnover in the hotel industry

	Equation 1	Equation 2
Total employment:		
50–99	−2.402 (2.39)	2.146 (.997)**
100–199	−1.717 (2.488)	2.71 (1.073)**
200+	−2.186 (2.591)	1.804 (1.203)
Proportion part-time	2.429 (1.952)	−2.303 (1.75)
Union presence	−.211 (1.027)	−1.693 (1.076)
Part of a chain	.536 (1.243)	1.498 (1.003)
Establishment age		
6–10 yrs	−.607 (.787)	−.263 (.773)
11–20 yrs	1.527 (1.002)	−.178 (.864)
20 yrs +	−1.083 (1.027)	.14 (.753)
Foreign owned	1.96 (.984)**	2.162 (.864)**
Personnel specialist present		−1.137 (.689)*
HR strategy	.1.206 (.854)	.79 (.876)
Attempt to introduce:		
technical change	.143 (.731)	.263 (.663)
organisational change	2.342 (.808)***	1.511 (.699)**
Formal personnel qualifications	.538 (.657)	
≥50% time spent on personnel issues	−1.411 (.957)	
Support staff present	.768 (.782)	
Labour turnover:		
20–40%		.056 (.809)
40–60%		.399 (.838)
60% +		1.676 (.977)*
Pseudo R^2	.292	.33
n	87	114

Notes: Dependent variable 1 = HRM, hotels 0 = non-HRM hotels.
Logit analysis. Coefficients given (standard errors in brackets).
All regressions control for region.
* significant at 10 per cent, ** significant at 5 per cent, *** significant at 1 per cent.

level personnel specialist may well be to deal with the recruitment and manpower planning needs created by high levels of labour turnover. This would lend support to the conclusions reached by Price (1994) and Lucas (1995, 1996) concerning the role of personnel specialists within the industry.

The question remains, however, as to who is responsible for championing the introduction of HRM if it is not unit-level personnel managers? The chief contenders are presumably unit-level general managers or, alternatively, regional or head office-level personnel. In the latter of these instances, HR policy and practice initiatives may be generated at head or regional office level and implemented top-down. The fact that HRM tends to be more sophisticated where hotels are part of a chain would suggest support for this interpretation. It therefore seems that within the hotel industry, the influence of regional or head office may well be important in terms of the introduction of a more sophisticated approach to HRM. While further questions relating to the nature of the relationship between unit-level hotels and head and regional offices can be addressed within the follow-up interviews, it would nevertheless seem, on the basis of the results achieved here, that where innovation has occurred, the involvement of unit-level personnel may well be somewhat limited.

The second equation in Table 4.4 looks at the relationship between labour turnover and HRM. In that it shows hotels with an annual labour turnover of greater than 60 per cent to be slightly more likely to have adopted an HRM approach than hotels with labour turnover of less than 20 per cent, this result is something of an anomaly. It could be explained in any one of three ways. Firstly, there may be a positive relationship between labour turnover and HRM, as hotels with high labour turnover have introduced HRM practices, albeit somewhat unsuccessfully, aimed at reducing turnover.

Secondly, there may a problem with missing data within this equation. Hotels classified as having adopted an HRM approach are more likely to have reported their labour turnover than are hotels that are not classified as having adopted such an approach. To be exact, 76.8 per cent of hotels classified as users of an HRM approach reported data on labour turnover compared with 69.05 per cent of hotels not classified as such, raising the possibility of non-response bias.

Thirdly, related to the previous point, it is possible that hotels adopting an HRM approach also take the monitoring of HR outcomes such as labour turnover more seriously. It may only be when effective monitoring takes place that the true extent of labour turnover is revealed. Where monitoring is nonexistent or less effective, respondents may underestimate the actual level of labour turnover within their hotels. Given these potential measurement problems, there are good reasons why this counter-intuitive finding should be treated with caution.

In sum, the following factors internal to the organisation stand out as important. Firstly, it seems that foreign-owned hotels have, on the whole, adopted a more sophisticated approach to the management of human resources than have UK-owned firms. Secondly, there has been a tendency for HRM to be introduced hand-in-hand with organisational change within the last six years. Finally, approaches to HRM tend to be slightly more sophisticated amongst chain hotels, and also amongst medium-sized hotels.

The impact of external factors

The results showing the relationship between factors external to the firm and the likelihood of an HRM approach having been adopted are presented in Table 4.5.

Concerning the insignificant variables, there is no relationship between product market stability and the likelihood of the hotel having adopted HRM. This finding, along with the fact that fewer than 8 per cent of the hotels within the sample describe their demand as seasonal and unpredictable, would suggest that seasonality can be discounted as a major logistical problem in hotels of the nature under investigation within this analysis.

The variables assessing the impact of the star rating of the hotel and the price charged for a standard double-room per night are also insignificant. Therefore, it is not only the more expensive hotels, or those with a four- or five-star rating as opposed to a one- to three-star rating, where HRM has a role to play.

The variables relating to the impact of decentralisation are also insignificant. In an attempt to test the thesis put forward by Purcell (1989) and Kirkpatrick, Davies and Oliver (1992) (discussed above), equations 4 and 5 of Table 4.5 show no negative relationship between the likelihood of HRM being practised at unit level and the extent of diversification within the organisation as a whole. Hotels that are part of a conglomerate are no less likely to have adopted HRM than are hotels that are part of a dominant business. This test may be somewhat superficial, as nothing is known as to the reasons why the organisations have diversified, or whether diversification has necessarily led to a weakening of the perceived importance of HRM at head office level. Moreover, innovation in individual hotels that are part of a conglomerate could be the result of local-level initiatives (local level in this instance referring to subsidiary or divisional level rather than unit level). Nevertheless, at least on the surface, the evidence presented here does not support the theory put forward by Purcell (1989) and Kirkpatrick, Davies and Oliver (1992).

The one external factor that stands out as a particularly important influence on HRM is the approach to business strategy the hotel has adopted. It is clear from equations 1 and 3 presented in Table 4.5 that an HRM approach is more likely to be found within hotels emphasising quality enhancement as the key to

Table 4.5 Relationship between external factors and HRM in the hotel industry

	Equation 1	Equation 2	Equation 3	Equation 4	Equation 5
Market seasonal but predictable	−.044 (.37)		−.15 (.384)	−.06 (.414)	−.072 (.406)
Market unpredictable	−.391 (.675)		−.409 (.684)	−.376 (.747)	−.407 (.74)
Quality enhancer	1.083 (.461)**		1.099 (.474)**	.986 (.504)**	1.086 (.496)**
'Stuck in the middle'	.815 (.487)*		.849 (.499)*	1.029 (.524)**	1.05 (.516)**
Four-star rating		−.38 (.441)	−.378 (.456)	−.268 (.511)	−.31 (.507)
Five-star rating		1.588 (1.306)	1.918 (1.367)	1.646 (1.44)	1.816 (1.419)
Price		.004 (.008)	.000 (.008)	−.002 (.009)	−.002 (.009)
Dominant business				.964 (.557)*	
Related business				.836 (.505)*	
Conglomerate				.734 (.609)	
Related/conglomerate exercising fairly/very high financial control				.062 (.401)	
Pseudo R^2	.071	.064	.093	.118	.098
n	157	157	157	141	141

Notes: Dependent variable 1 = HRM hotels, 0= non-HRM hotels.
Logit analysis. Coefficients given (standard errors in brackets).
All regressions control for region.
* significant at 10 per cent, ** significant at 5 per cent.

business strategy than within hotels emphasising cost reduction. This provides clear support for the matching model presented by Schuler (1989) and Schuler and Jackson (1987), and also for the arguments raised within the hotel industry literature by Haywood (1983), Lewis (1987), Mattsson (1994) and Nightingale (1985), that an HRM approach is more likely to be viewed as important where the establishment is focusing on quality enhancement within its competitive strategy.

Table 4.6 Relationship between internal and external factors and HRM in the hotel industry

Total employment:	
50–99	.495 (.809)
100–199	1.187 (.822)
200+	.549 (1.026)
Proportion of workforce part-time	.154 (1.153)
Union presence	−1.297 (.797)
Part of a chain	1.129 (.674)*
Age:	
6–10 years	−.417 (.571)
11–20 years	.205 (.655)
20+ years	.089 (.596)
Foreign owned	1.153 (.624)*
Personnel specialist	−.206 (.497)
HR strategy	.659 (.558)
Attempt to introduce:	
Technical change	.497 (.478)
Organisational change	1.062 (.499)**
Market unstable but predictable	−.266 (.468)
Market unstable and unpredictable	−.365 (.785)
Quality enhancer	1.186 (.539)**
'Stuck in the middle'	1.054 (.596)*
Price	.003 (.01)
Four-star	−.471 (.551)
Five-star	1.311 (1.536)
Pseudo R^2	.233
n	157

Notes: Dependent variable 1 = HRM hotels, 0 = non-HRM hotels.
Logit analysis. Coefficients given (standard errors in brackets).
All regressions control for region.
* significant at 10 per cent, ** significant at 5 per cent.

Internal and external factors – which are the more influential?

Table 4.6 reports an equation that includes both the internal and external independent variables under consideration so far. The results demonstrate that there are both internal and external influences that operate independently of each other. Firstly, in line with situational contingency or matching models, the usage of HRM is higher amongst hotels emphasising quality enhancement within their business strategies. Secondly, chain hotels and foreign-owned hotels are more likely to have adopted HRM, irrespective of the business strategy pursued. Also irrespective of the approach taken to business strategy, there has been a tendency for HRM to be introduced hand-in-hand with organisational change.

Discussions and conclusions

The aim here has been to test the influence of a range of factors both internal and external to the organisation put forward in both the hotel industry literature and also within the generic HRM literature.

In the event, several of the potential internal influences on HRM had very little or no effect whatsoever. Workforce resistance to change does not seem to have a major influence, neither does the proportion of the workforce working part-time (a finding which suggests that the daily fluctuations in demand within the hotel industry do not present major logistical problems in terms of the introduction of HRM). The weak unions within the industry would also seem to have little influence on policy choice. Looking at personnel managers, their presence appears to be unrelated to the introduction of HRM, irrespective of how well qualified they are, how much time they spend working on employ-ment-related issues and how many support staff they have. Their primary role may well have more to do with the manpower planning requirements arising from high levels of labour turnover. It seems probable, therefore, that HRM innovation has been championed at either regional or head office level rather than by unit-level personnel.

Turning to factors internal to the firm that are related to the adoption of an HRM approach, two internal factors stand out within the analysis as being particularly important. Firstly, an HRM approach is more likely to have been adopted where management has attempted a major organisational change within the last six years or since operations began. This suggests firstly, that an HRM approach has been introduced as part of an overall package of organisa-tional change, possibly involving delayering and new organisational structures.

It also suggests that the adoption of HRM may be quite a recent phenomenon within the hotel industry.

The second internal factor that stands out relates to ownership, the evidence suggesting that foreign-owned hotels have adopted more sophisticated approaches to HRM than have UK-owned hotels. In addition, there is a slight suggestion that amongst chain hotels the adoption of HRM is more likely. This would seem to be explained by the fact that HR issues are more likely to be considered to be a senior management concern within these hotels than within independent hotels.

Turning to external factors, market instability, which does not appear to be particularly high (with only 7.64 per cent of hotels reporting their demand to be seasonal and unpredictable, compared with 50.96 per cent who describe demand as stable), does not have any particular influence on the approach taken to HRM. Seasonality, it seems, can be discounted as a major determinant of the approaches taken to HRM within hotels of this nature.

By contrast, the approach taken to business strategy would appear to be a highly influential determinant of the approach taken to HRM. The results here clearly demonstrate that HRM is more widespread amongst hotels where service quality enhancement is emphasised as the key component within business strategy than amongst hotels where cost reduction is viewed as central. It would appear, therefore, that where managers within the industry have realised the importance of service quality, they have also realised the importance of the adoption of an HRM approach.

Finally, the analysis within this chapter suggests that the factors influencing HRM decision-making within the hotel industry are no different from the factors influencing HRM decision-making elsewhere. The conclusion reached within Chapter 2 was that very few of the influences on HRM policy choice discussed within the hotel industry literature are in fact unique to the industry. The empirical analysis conducted here demonstrates that the impact of these few unique influences is minimal, with instability of demand and labour turn-over having little or no impact on the approach taken to HRM. By contrast, business strategy, national ownership and being part of a chain all exert a major influence. All of these factors are also considered important within the mainstream literature. As such, the results do not support the argument that the hotel industry is in any way 'different', or subject to a unique set of contingencies not faced by managers in other industries.

The following chapter examines the HRM practices adopted within a selection of hotels in closer detail, assessing in particular whether the hotels categorised as 'HRM hotels' within this chapter are deserving of their title, and whether there is substance behind the widely reported rhetoric of HRM reported within Chapter 3. Finally, one of the key explanatory variables within the analysis presented in this chapter relates to business strategy. This is also a key variable within the analysis of outcomes reported in Chapter 6, and as such is worthy of further investigation and verification. The following chapter therefore provides an assessment of the validity of the 'quality enhancer', 'cost reducer' and 'other' classifications.

Note

1   The intention was also to include a variable looking at the proportion of temporary workers. However, this has been omitted, as there is a question mark concerning the quality of the data collected within the survey. Respondents were asked to state the number of employees on fixed-term or casual contracts of 12 months or less in duration. Many responded by saying that the entire workforce fell within this category. Given the probability that this variable has been misinterpreted, it is omitted from the analysis.

5 HRM in practice in the hotel industry

This chapter focuses on a series of interviews conducted between September and November 1996 as a follow-up to the 1995 Survey of Human Resource Management in the Hotel Industry. As discussed at the end of the preceding chapter, these interviews were conducted primarily to test the validity of the variable used to define 'HRM' and 'non-HRM' hotels. 'HRM' hotels were defined as those using above the mean number of HRM practices asked about (in other words, at least 14 out of 22), and also claiming to deliberately integrate their HR practices with each other. Is it the case that the hotels falling into this category merit their 'HRM' title?

Secondly, the follow-up interviews aim to provide support for the business strategy typology constructed in the previous chapter. This is a highly important predictor of the extent to which HRM is being practised, and as such it is worthy of further validation. How far is 'quality enhancement' or 'cost reduction' a fair description of the priorities within the business strategies of the hotels classified as such? The emphases within the business strategies of the hotels classified as 'other' will also be examined in further detail.

Thirdly, in that the follow-up interviews involve a more in-depth analysis of the practices introduced within each of the hotels, the manner in which they function and the spirit in which they were intended, further corroboration will be possible in relation to the results presented in Chapter 3 concerning the extent of usage of HRM in the industry. As discussed in Chapter 2, Hales (1987) received highly positive responses to his questionnaire examining the introduction of quality of working-life practices, but in his follow-up interviews, he found that many of the practices introduced were aimed solely at management, and were aimed at labour intensification and job loading. Hales (1987) also found a general belief amongst management that staff were not interested in accepting greater responsibility. A similar finding here will cast serious doubt on the conclusions reached in chapter three in relation to the nature and extent of usage of HRM within the industry.

Finally, it will also be possible within the follow-up interviews to shed further light on the factors that influence managerial decision-making in relation to HRM discussed in the previous chapter. For example, the results in Chapter 4 would seem to suggest that sophisticated approaches to HRM are more in evidence within chain hotels. The follow-up interviews will enable an assessment of the relationship between corporate and regional headquarters and individual units, in terms of the extent to which HRM practices have emanated from regional or head offices, as opposed to having been developed at unit level. An analysis of the extent to which the hotel industry workforce is as willing to accept change as implied within the analysis in the previous chapter will also be possible, as will an evaluation of the attitudes of interviewees towards trade unions.

Hotels were selected for inclusion within the follow-up interview programme as follows. Firstly, given the importance of business strategy as a predictor of the extent to which HRM has been introduced, the sample was split into 'cost reducers', 'quality enhancers' and 'others'. Each of these sub-samples was then split into 'HRM organisations' and 'non-HRM organisations', using the definition adopted in the previous chapter. As such, six categories were created, these being 'HRM cost reducers', 'non-HRM cost reducers', 'HRM quality enhancers', 'non-HRM quality enhancers', 'HRM others' and 'non-HRM others'. One hotel was then selected from each category. To maintain consistency, all the selected hotels were part of a chain, were non-union and had attempted a major organisational change in the last six years. All interviewees were designated personnel specialists.

Given the amount of the interviewee's time that extensive follow-up interviews take, the willingness of managers to take part in the interview programme was in itself surprising. In the event, only one manager refused to be interviewed point blank. From a methodological point of view, this is important, as there is no reason why the hotels visited should be considered unrepresentative of the categories from which they have been selected.

The next section addresses each of the case-study interviews in turn, considering in particular whether the HRM categorisation and the business strategy typology are justified.

The 'non-HRM cost reducer'

The 'non-HRM cost reducer' hotel is located in central London and is part of a small family-owned chain. The underlying philosophy of the hotel, which employs 115 staff, emphasises the efficient management of staffing levels and cost control. Staffing levels are set and agreed by the senior management team, and variations in demand for labour are dealt with using casual staff, who receive no contract of employment and no sick pay or pension entitlements. About 50 per cent of food service staff are casual workers passing through the UK, maybe spending six months there at most. Typically, they have careers in their home countries and have come to the UK to learn English. These employees are trained to a level necessary to provide a certain level of service, but they are provided with no further training beyond this.

There is no evidence of single status terms and conditions of employment, despite claims to the contrary within the questionnaire. Management staff receive more benefits than do non-management staff, but operate on an 'hours-as-required' basis, whereas staff up to supervisory level work 40 hours per week plus paid overtime. Concerning the pension scheme, managers are able to join from day one. Non-management staff, by contrast, have to wait a year. Management are eligible for private healthcare. Non-management staff are not. All employees, including casuals, are appraised every six months. Recruitment is carried out primarily via word-of-mouth or via internal advertisements within the group. Selection is on the basis of interviews, there being no use of selection tests, although all new staff go through a one-day induction.

Ninety-five per cent of training over and above customer care courses for front-line staff and hygiene training for waiters and chefs, in line with statutory requirements, is on the job. Many of the staff are seen as unwilling to take on extra responsibilities or to be trained or developed, and developmental training tends to be reserved for supervisory staff. Nevertheless, there are opportunities to progress for operative staff demonstrating aptitude and a positive attitude.

Attempts have been made recently to improve communications within the hotel. Information is cascaded down the organisation via memos and notice-boards and via head of department meetings and departmental meetings. Bi-weekly meetings are held between departmental representatives and either the general manager or other department heads. These meetings provide another forum whereby problems can be discussed as and when they arise. The hotel operates an 'open-door' management policy, and the majority of managers are known to staff by their first names. This is considered effective to a degree, the personnel manager commenting "…we tend to find that generally, if people have got problems they will discuss them at any time…"

Despite the not inconsiderable number of communication and consultation forums, key decisions are nevertheless often made unilaterally by management. For example, during the recessionary early 1990s, following discussions at senior management level and checks on the legality of the proposals, sickness benefit provision was reduced as a cost cutting measure without any consultation with staff. As the personnel manager commented:

> ...even if they [the staff] had a problem with it, it still happened, because we were giving them the required contractual notice of change of terms...

Although it is only in the field of communication where any major changes to HRM practices have been made in recent years, the hotel nevertheless has Investors in People accreditation. Accreditation was sought in part to attempt to attract higher calibre staff, although the personnel manager expressed the sentiment that the quality of staff at the hotel was not as high as perhaps it could be, commenting:

> ...there's still a lot of people who don't care what we do, as long as we look after them...feed them, give them a uniform and give them their pay...

Overall, the 'non-HRM' label attached to this hotel would seem to be justified. The interview also supports the picture painted within the questionnaire in relation to the practices that have been adopted by the hotel. Only with reference to the single status issue did the hotel claim to be operating a policy that in reality it was not.

However, while the 'non-HRM' label would appear to be accurate, what of the 'cost reducer' label? When questioned on this issue, the personnel manager commented:

> ...we will provide a quality product and a very good service for the price we are offering...cost control is very important – large accounts will move for the sake of £5 a night...

HR policies are geared to meet the needs of this 'bottom line' approach. Wage increases and wage costs in particular are tightly controlled. Heads of departments are given budgets and they are required to forecast wage costs each week. This is compared with expected revenue in order to generate a wage percentage. If it is too high, department heads have to find a way to reduce labour costs (in other words, shed a few casual staff). A conscious decision has been taken to increase the number of casual workers in order that headcount can be matched more closely to peaks and troughs in demand. The 'cost reducer' label therefore seems justified.

On both business strategy and the approach taken to HRM, the question-naire paints a fairly accurate picture where the 'non-HRM cost reducer' is concerned.

The 'HRM cost reducer'

The 'HRM cost reducer', which employs 130 staff and is located in central London, is part of a large international chain. It was awarded Investors in People accreditation in September 1995. Is its label as an 'HRM hotel' justified?

The hotel is currently going through several considerable changes, though it already displays many of the practices commonly associated with an HRM approach. Turning firstly to job design, the hotel is moving away from the use of job descriptions to job profiles, with the intention of increasing functional flexibility. One example of this is in housekeeping. The hotel is looking to launch a 'Keymaids' programme. Under this programme, chambermaids will be responsible for their own floor, and they will deal not only with traditional chambermaiding tasks, but also with maintenance and paperwork. Supervisors will randomly spot check a couple, rather than all of the rooms.

The expectation is that the introduction of the 'Keymaids' concept will take time. Other hotels within the group have already introduced it, though it has taken 12 to 18 months for the system to be installed, because of the extent of training that has had to take place, and the need to overcome fears emanating from expanded job roles. At this hotel, there are similar concerns in relation to training, particularly where maintenance and the paperwork the maids will be responsible for are concerned. Nevertheless, it is hoped that when intro-duced, the 'Keymaids' concept will raise the status of the job, and also result in higher pay levels, as it is generally accepted that maids will have to be paid more, to reflect the wider range of skills necessary to perform the job.

Attempts are also being made to empower front-line operative staff. The realisation of the need for this stems from the experiences of senior head office managers, all of whom are expected as part of their ongoing training and develop-ment to spend short periods of time working within an operative role. Their experiences have led them to realise that unless front-line staff have the authority to solve non-routine problems as and when they arise, customer impressions of quality and professionalism at the point of service delivery will be impaired. Many examples of empowerment in action are small – for example, being able to deal quickly with queries related to billing, or offering to hail a taxi for customers who are checking out and are in a hurry – but they can make a tremendous difference to the customer's perception of the quality of service.

For such an approach to operate effectively, the need for managers to play a 'coaching' rather than a 'controlling' role has been realised, such that if a member of staff makes a mistake, they are encouraged to see it as a learning experience. The interviewee stressed that managers have taken on board that they must allow operative staff to use their discretion, and that they must ensure staff have the confidence that supervisors trust them to act alone.

The adoption of such an approach has led to a series of other changes in relation to HR practices within the hotel. For example, where recruitment is concerned, emphasis is now placed on identifying the candidates most likely to be prepared to use their own discretion and judgement. Displaying the right attitude is seen as more important than possessing technical skills. In line with this ethos, behavioural tests are being developed for recruitment to non-managerial positions. These tests aim to assess, for example, the ability of applicants to work in a team and whether the applicant has the requisite personality to work in a service delivery position. Concerning recruitment to managerial positions, 'behavioural event interviews' are used. The hotels group is soon to introduce assessment centres for recruitment to supervisory positions and above.

Training and development has also assumed greater importance. The personnel manager aims to ensure that everybody, no matter how short a time they spend in the hotel, will leave having learned something new. The emphasis on the role of department heads as coaches and trainers has increased, as has the need to involve as trainers a range of both non-managerial as well as managerial staff. On the new off-the-job customer care course, for example, non-management staff noted for particularly high work standards have been given the responsibility of providing training to other staff. Other training initiatives under development include a resource centre equipped with CD-ROM, foreign language training courses and job-swaps between hotels within the group. The hotel also sponsors staff on an ad-hoc basis to attend courses outside the hotel. Reflecting the 'continuous development' ethos, efforts are made to ensure that the highest possible proportion of promotions are made internally, with vacancies within the group as far afield as the Middle East and Africa being advertised monthly.

Performance appraisals have been introduced to assess individual training needs, and to identify the staff most likely to respond to developmental training. Appraisals also provide a mechanism by which HRM practices can be integrated with the group's business strategy. Staff are appraised on six 'critical practices'. These are aimed at the achievement of the individual department's and the hotel's 'Statement of Purpose', which in turn is derived from the UK and regional 'Statement of Purpose'. The 'Statement of Purpose' at this hotel stresses:

> ...leading the way in best business practice and innovative concepts ...providing a communicative environment for our employees, to train and develop their skills and recognise opportunities for advancement...

The statement then continues by emphasising:

> ...improved quality standards, increased guest delight and a growth in hotel profit...

The 'critical practices', or role behaviours required to achieve the goals specified within the 'Statement of Purpose' are first, the need to be outgoing; second, to always look for ways to improve service delivery and not to provide any service which is not up to standard; third, to always be a team player; fourth, to personally see through service delivery; fifth to identify service delivery problems and resolve the situation even where it is not the individual's specific job role, and finally, to take an organised approach to work. By focusing training and development, recruitment, job design and communication on the achievement of these six 'critical practices' HR strategy and HR practices can be consciously designed to achieve the goals within the hotel's 'Statement of Purpose'.

Finally, concerning terms and conditions, most, but not all status differences between management and non-management staff have been removed. Holiday entitlement and the pension scheme is common to both management and non-management staff. Non-management staff have a slightly different medical scheme, however. Concerning hours of work, heads of department and certain supervisors work on an 'hours-as-required' basis, whereas operative level staff work 40 hours per week plus paid overtime. Performance-related pay based on performance appraisal has been introduced recently. This is seen as a method by which commitment and high achievement can be rewarded.

There is no doubt that the hotel in question is worthy of its 'HRM' title. What, however, of its classification as a 'cost reducer'? It is clear within the hotel's statement of purpose and the critical practices (within which cost control is not mentioned once), that this hotel would fit more comfortably within the quality enhancer category.

As mentioned earlier, this hotel is undergoing considerable transformation, and one part of this transformation is an increasing emphasis on the services that add value to the product offered by the hotel. In line with this, a great deal of low-rate business has been shed. Nevertheless, at the time of the survey, the respondent rightly highlighted the emphasis on price competition.

Therefore, this hotel further demonstrates the 'HRM' category to have been appropriately defined. The hotel displays many of the policies and practices and an underlying ethos in line with an HRM approach. This provides further support for the conclusions reached in Chapter 3 relating to the extent of usage of HRM. There is no evidence that the practices asked about in the questionnaire have been misinterpreted by the respondent, and the practices the respondent claimed were in operation at the time of the survey were, in the event, operating within the hotel as expected.

The 'non-HRM quality enhancer'

The follow-up interview within this hotel, which employs 98 staff, further confirms the validity of the categorisations adopted in the previous chapter. In line with its 'non-HRM' label, this hotel displayed very few of the characteristics associated with an HRM approach. For example, there has been no conscious effort to remove status differences between management and non-management staff, and there is no usage of behavioural selection tests during recruitment. Upward communication seems to be left to chance, the personnel manager commenting:

> ...we hope that people are not afraid to come forward to talk to us...

Training is provided in three areas, these being technical training, customer service training and off-the-job training, which includes college and management courses. There is also the opportunity for one staff member from the hotel per year to attend a four-week course at Cornell University. In addition, the hotel organises work placements overseas. External college courses, advertised on a noticeboard within the hotel, are available to anybody. However, it is not the case that training needs are identified in any systematic way. Training is provided to those who show an interest. As the personnel manager commented:

> ...providing opportunities must encourage people. Whether they actually take advantage of them is a different matter. You can buy someone a ticket, but you can't actually put them on the train...

It seems that there is no formal mechanism to systematically identify those who require remedial training, or those who have the potential to benefit from developmental training.

The hotel extensively recruits casuals from Germany and France. They come to the hotel on year-long contracts, with the primary aim of improving English language skills, but they bring with them the skills they have learned during their apprenticeships in their home countries. As such, they are seen as compensating for the poor quality of applicants drawn from the domestic jobs market. They fill a wide range of positions, from reception and restaurant positions to management roles.

No attempts have been made to redesign jobs to enhance staff motivation or flexibility. On this issue, the personnel manager commented:

> ...if somebody wants a change of jobs for example, they will come and ask, can I go and work in so-and-so? We're very simple, very primitive in that sense. People know their jobs and they are not complicated. There isn't a complicated job in the hotel...

Similarly, no attempts have been made to decentralise authority. With reference to the concept of empowerment, the personnel manager commented:

> ...do you keep control of the business if you allow a waitress to replace somebody's complaint, let's say their steak, without calling the manager? I would say no...

Reflective of this approach is the hotel's 'quickfire message system' whereby, if an employee receives a complaint they do not have the authority to deal with themselves, they must immediately find a manager to handle it. There has been no decentralisation of authority such that complaints or queries can be dealt with at source by front-line staff.

The hotel's 'non-HRM' label is clearly justified. The personnel manager nevertheless stressed, as within the questionnaire, the importance of service quality, commenting that customers are willing to pay extra for high standards of service, particularly in terms of interactions with staff, the personal nature of the service and the ability to deal with requests in a professional manner. To achieve the requisite service quality, 'hotel people' (to use the personnel manager's phrase, "...people who get pleasure from serving...") are targeted during recruitment. Candidates are assessed in interviews on their former work experience, presentation and their communication and interpersonal skills (these being judged on intuition during interviews). Beyond this, eliciting the staff commitment necessary to achieve the required service standards seems to be left to chance:

> …most people know what's right. They know their job, and management gets the standard of performance it will accept … and management here does not accept second best…

Motivation is not something that can be achieved though HR policies and practices, in the opinion of the personnel manager:

> …motivation is from within. You can lead by example, motivate them, marginally, but for how long?

How effective the hotel is in achieving its quality enhancer goals is open to question. Of the 5 per cent of guest questionnaire replies expressing dissatisfaction, many complaints concerned staff-related issues rather than technical issues such as faulty equipment in rooms, as highlighted by the following quote from the hotel's 1994 'manifesto':

> …[guests] complained of incidents which could have well been prevented if the staff involved had acted with greater observance or tact in their personal exchange with the guest. The consequence of poor attention to detail is that the guest leaves the hotel with the impression that we don't care – thereby undoing all the good conscientious work that is done most of the time. Staff who allow their personal feelings to show by being too abrupt also leave the guest feeling that their comfort and welfare is of little concern.

Service quality enhancement is clearly seen as more important than competition on price, thus suggesting the categorisation of this hotel within the 'quality enhancer' category as valid. However, the 'non-HRM' label attached to this hotel also seems to be valid. Although the hotel offers opportunities for training, there is no formal mechanism whereby those in need of training, or those most likely to benefit from a developmental approach can be identified. Jobs are not designed in such a way that employees would be able to put their skills into practice on returning to work, and there is no evidence that staff capable of career progression are being systematically developed and offered promotion opportunities.

The 'HRM quality enhancer'

This hotel, employing 140 staff, is part of a national chain of hotels, which in turn, is part of an international hotel group. It is located on the outskirts of Milton Keynes and has Investors in People accreditation.

In the questionnaire, the personnel manager claimed to operate all but five of the HRM practices asked about, a picture that on the whole was confirmed by the follow-up interview, suggesting the description of this hotel as an 'HRM' hotel to be accurate. However, there seemed to be some confusion over the issue of single status. There was little evidence that status differences between management and non-management staff had been removed, despite the fact that the hotel claimed to have harmonised terms and conditions. For example, management are eligible for private health insurance and also a bonus scheme, whereas staff are not.

Otherwise, the picture painted by the questionnaire was verified by the follow-up interview. Looking firstly at recruitment, emphasis is placed upon the selection of applicants with an aptitude for customer service. Past experience or qualifications are seen as important, but not as important as the right attitude. However, the view was that 'the right attitude' could be spotted at interview, with psychometric or behavioural tests not being used.

Induction into the hotel is extensive. On arrival, new recruits are put through a standard company induction, which introduces them to the hotel's mission statement, and the importance of customer service. New recruits also undergo 'regional orientation', where they are taken to another hotel to walk a 'customer's journey'. Cross-functional co-operation and team building is also emphasised within the off-the-job commercial hospitality course, which all new staff undergo within their first six months. The aim is to encourage staff to view the hotel as a unit rather than as a collection of discrete functions. Employees from different functions, both management and non-management, are deliberately brought together to help develop an understanding of the problems that arise in other areas, and the ways in which different functions can support each other.

Multi-skilling and cross-functional flexibility is extensive, both within and between departments. Staff move between front of house and food and beverage quite freely. For example, it is not unusual for reception staff to wait on tables if a major conference or banqueting function is taking place. Inter-functional 'cross-exposure' training is also seen as an important part of the team-building process. An example of this is the 'cross-exposure' between accounts and reception. The accounts function starts with reception, where billing is handled. In the past, errors made by the front desk have created difficulties for accounts, damaging relationships between the two departments. Deliberate 'cross-exposure' between these two departments has enabled those in accounts to experience and appreciate the problems encountered by reception, and has enabled receptionists to appreciate the impact of errors on the accounts department. In a similar vein, housekeeping supervisors also spend time on reception, as these two functions also work together closely.

Job design initiatives do not end with cross-functional flexibility. There have recently been attempts to decentralise responsibility and authority to lower grade staff. In dealing with customer complaints, the aim has been to give front-line staff as much responsibility or 'ownership' as possible, to deal with customer complaints as far as they can on their own, rather than passing the complaint on to the duty manager. For example, receptionists now have the authority to deal with queries over bills, and it is within their authority to remove items from the bill if they feel a complaint is justified. In the restaurant, staff are given the authority to provide customers with dishes on the house in order to compensate for a complaint. Previously, only duty managers would have had the authority to take such action.

In terms of communication, the hotel has introduced consultative committees that look at ways in which the running of the hotel can be improved. These are attended by elected representatives from each department, as well as the general manager and the personnel manager. Any points of dissatisfaction or ideas for improvement, however small, can be raised here. The hotel also operates annual 'Talkback' attitude surveys (conducted at group rather than unit level), aimed at eliciting the workforce's views on a range of issues such as terms and conditions of employment, the appraisal system, the amount of communication and training. On the basis of the results, each hotel develops a six-point plan relating to areas of improvement in the coming year.

Each employee is appraised on a yearly basis. Objectives and areas of development are jointly agreed within the appraisal interview. After six months, there is a follow-up 'semi' appraisal, to assess whether those objectives are being met, and whether further objectives can be set. Appraisals are currently not linked to merit pay, though this may happen in the near future. In addition, the appraisal system is used to facilitate succession planning, in that the appraisals enable the identification and development of staff with the ability and inclination to progress through the organisation. Promotion is from within whenever possible. As such, some staff have progressed very quickly career-wise. The assistant restaurant manager for example, was recruited initially as a casual only two years ago, and has subsequently been promoted through the ranks. This is just one example of the not uncommon rapid career progression for those who demonstrate potential.

The hotel has clearly developed a range of sophisticated HR practices over the past few years, and as such the 'HRM' label appears accurate. When questioned on the 'quality enhancer' underlying philosophy within the business strategy, the personnel manager commented:

> ...I think that overrides everything to be honest ... it's something that is really preached to the staff, and they all try to live by it...

The personnel manager also claims not inconsiderable success in achieving the 'outstanding customer service' goal laid down within the hotel's mission statement:

> ...the staff are fantastic here in the way in which they deal with people. Staff from other hotels like to come here and be seen to be the best at what they do...

As such, the categorisation of this hotel in the previous chapter firstly as an 'HRM hotel' and secondly as a 'quality enhancer' would seem to be justified.

The 'non-HRM other'

The Manchester-based 'non-HRM other' employs 240 staff and is one of a large worldwide chain of international hotels. Although originally categorised as a 'non-HRM' hotel within the questionnaire, a range of practices associated with an HRM approach were found to be in operation. There are two possible reasons for this discrepancy. Firstly, the hotel is undergoing considerable change, and as such, several new practices had been introduced since the time the questionnaire was conducted. Secondly, within the questionnaire, the question relating to trainability as a major selection criterion was left blank, though in the event, it should have been answered in the affirmative. Also, the single status question was correctly answered in the negative (the only hotel to do this, despite the fact that extensive moves had been made to harmonise terms and conditions). This may have been enough for this hotel to be classified as 'non-HRM' on the basis of the definition adopted within the previous chapter.

Turning to business strategy issues, the respondent emphasised responsiveness to customer needs, providing a distinctive service and value for money within the questionnaire. As such, the hotel did not automatically fit either the cost reducer or the quality enhancer definition. Further questioning in the follow-up interview, however, suggested service quality to be a key emphasis within the hotel's business strategy.

In terms of the achievement of service quality goals, the conclusion has been reached within the hotel group that it is necessary to empower those people within the organisation who deliver the service, in other words, operative-level staff. Examples of empowerment include the project – still in its infancy – to get rid of scripts specifying a series of questions that must be asked to the guest on arrival. Getting rid of such scripts enables staff to use their judgement over what to say to new arrivals, and how brief or extensive to make the inter-change. For example, if a queue is forming, or if a guest is noticeably tired, it is preferable to keep the interchange brief. These are contingencies that receptionists can spot, and are capable of judging. The aim is to harness this judgement and enable service delivery to be tailored to specific situations.

Such empowerment is still embryonic, and certain decisions, such as the discounts staff should be allowed to offer, are yet to be made. Nevertheless, there is an awareness amongst managers that they must allow staff to make mistakes without fear of sanctions. In the past, management style has been a problem, and the personnel manager admits that there are still quite a few 'traditionalists' within the group. However, the new general manager develop-ment programme, which has run over the last three years, is viewed as instru-mental in the development of a less control-oriented management approach. Although the programme is aimed at the upgrading of a range of business skills relating to finance, sales and marketing, human resource issues are also heavily emphasised. As such, the managers who complete this course have tended to be more open to innovative ideas in relation to HRM. Secondly, on a separate issue, the programme has also presented an opportunity for women to reach general management positions, as line managers from all disciplines are recruited to the programme. The traditional route into general management in the past was via the male-dominated food and beverage functions. Female managers in the industry have tended to cluster within the sales and personnel functions, and as such have typically been overlooked in terms of promotion to general manager posts.

The decentralised approach emphasised by empowerment is also reflected within the 'continuous service improvement programme', which involves departmental meetings held once a week that look at complaints from duty/ senior managers' log books, and ways of avoiding them in the future.

As well as attempts to empower lower-level staff, efforts have also been made to improve flexibility and multi-skilling. Previously, job descriptions were narrower, for example recruitment would be to the restaurant or to the bar, rather than to the food and beverage function as a whole. However, food and beverage 'hosts', who are trained in the skills necessary to work in the dining room, the lounge and in room service, have been introduced. Often, one of these areas is busier than the others, so multi-skilling enables staff to move around as required. More recently, multi-skilling has been introduced into the front office, such that a receptionist is now trained to work as a concierge, on the switchboard, in food and beverage co-ordination, in reservations or in sales. To facilitate this process, these functions have all been moved into one area within the hotel. Staff are reported as being positive about multi-skilling:

> …we found the staff like it, because generally, it gives them more strings to their bow and it makes the job more interesting…

A further benefit of multi-skilling is that it enables a leaner operation:

> …previously what we were doing was getting casuals in because we might be short in one particular area, even though we would have people standing around in another area…

Although it is difficult to separate out the exact cause and effect, as other changes were taking place at the same time, part of the 10 per cent fall in labour turnover the hotel has experienced is accredited to the introduction of this style of working.

The policy of multi-skilling and empowering the workforce has had considerable knock-on effects on recruitment and training. As the personnel manager commented:

> …if you are going to get people who are empowered you have got to make sure you are recruiting the right person in the first place, so you have to concentrate much more on the personality aspects than on the technical side … but you have also got to assess whether they have got the sort of mental agility, because they have to be fairly responsive to customers who ask a question, and not just say "I'll go and get the duty manager", so you are looking for a more educated person…

There is also a focus within recruitment on attitude rather than on skill, particularly at operative level. Behavioural testing is carried out for operative grades, and psychometric tests are used for management grades. Assessment centres are being extended beyond the selection of graduates to selection to other positions also. On an *ad hoc* basis, school leavers, if they show interest in working in the industry, might be invited to spend a short period of time working within the hotel in order that they can experience hotel life first hand. Graduates with a non-hotel and catering degree who show an interest in working in the industry have also been offered these opportunities in the past.[1]

Once staff have been selected, the hotel operates a day-long formal induction, during which staff are introduced to the company's procedures, policies and values. Staff are formally appraised at the end of their probationary period and 'personal business objectives' (relating to training or skills acquisition for example) are set.

As such, the hotel goes to considerable lengths to ensure the recruitment of those with the requisite ability and attitude to function effectively within a multi-skilled and 'empowered' environment. However, it has been acknowledged that higher calibre employees come at a price. Attempts are therefore being made to encourage the head office to increase pay rates. A pay and benefits working party has been set up, the minimum rate has been increased, and the working party is now looking at increasing rates higher up the pay scale in order to restore differentials. The impact on the overall payroll throughout the group will be considerable. The expectation is that the raising of salaries will take place in a step-by-step manner, possibly over a five-year period. Nevertheless, there is an appreciation that pay increases are necessary to attract employees of the requisite calibre to the hotel.

The need for a functionally flexible, 'empowered' approach has also had an impact on the approach taken towards training. As well as training staff in a range of functional skills, staff have also undergone 'positive influencing' and 'interaction management' courses, to help them develop their interpersonal skills and to be able to deal with situations on their own. Performance appraisals are instrumental in identifying those who require training. They are also used for succession planning, in particular, to select staff for developmental training if they show the requisite interest and potential. Indeed, there are considerable career opportunities for those at operative level. All vacancies are advertised locally, and 50 per cent of these vacancies are filled from within. This has been the case for the last 3 to 4 years and has been accredited to the heavier emphasis on developmental training within the appraisal system, which has made managers more aware of the capabilities and aspirations of their staff. Self-appraisal has recently been introduced whereby operatives appraise themselves prior to the appraisal meeting with their supervisor.

The hotel has also made efforts to minimise status differences between management and non-management staff, with the introduction of a sick-pay scheme for non-management staff, and the introduction of the same pension scheme for staff as is available to managers. This is further seen as necessary to aid recruitment of higher calibre staff. Everyone is paid direct into their bank accounts on a fortnightly basis. The only difference in terms and conditions still in existence concerns the bonus scheme, within which management tend to receive a larger percentage (10 per cent of salary as opposed to 2.5 per cent for graded staff last year).

This follow-up interview casts slight doubt on the validity of the classification of HRM and non-HRM organisations used in the previous chapter. Nevertheless, it further validates the conclusions reached within the Chapter 3, in that it provides a further example of substance behind the rhetoric of HRM.

The 'HRM other'

This hotel employs 217 staff, is located within central London, and is part of a national chain of hotels, which in turn is part of an international group. Investors in People accreditation was achieved in May 1996. Within the questionnaire, the respondent gave more positive responses than any other respondent within the follow-up interview programme, answering in the negative only to the questions concerning the use of psychological tests and whether there is an explicit policy in relation to formal training. In the event, while the picture painted within the questionnaire is somewhat exaggerated, this hotel was nevertheless correctly categorised as an 'HRM' hotel.

The major discrepancy within the questionnaire replies related to single status terms and conditions arrangements. In common with four of the previous five case-study hotels, the respondent at this hotel claimed single status to be in operation, which in the event was not the case. While holiday entitlements and sick pay provision were the same, pension provision, healthcare arrangements and hours of work were not. The misinterpretation of the single status issue has proved to be a common theme within all but one of the follow-up interviews.

In other respects, the hotel is operating quite a sophisticated package of HR techniques. But what of the business strategy these techniques are designed to complement? On the basis of the questionnaire responses, this hotel was categorised as 'other', though in the event, the hotel's business strategy would have fitted comfortably into the 'quality enhancer' category, service quality being an obvious focus within the hotel. On this issue the personnel manager commented:

> ...to be successful you have to have that little bit extra to give the guests, the 'magic' that no other hotel gives ... that extra smile, using their name, the way we answer the telephone ... are all noticeable and are picked up on by the guest...

Service quality is undeniably seen as the key to success, as is developing an understanding of what the customer sees as important:

> ...customer needs are changing all the time ... you have to be responsive to that ... guest comments have to be discussed, so we know exactly what the customer wants...

The manner in which human resources are managed is central to the achievement of the 'magic' described above. When asked what makes the business successful, the personnel manager replied:

> ...the people ... the way people look after their staff, the way they are introduced to the business, the way they are trained, the way they are communicated to...

This is reflected within the HR practices in operation at the hotel. In relation to recruitment and selection, the most important criterion is attitude. Applicants with a customer service focus and those with an appreciation for what the job entails are selected on the basis of their role-play responses within behavioural situation interviews. All potential new recruits are made aware of the job descriptions during the selection stage.

Once recruited, a considerable emphasis is placed on formal induction. New staff attend an induction programme within the hotel they have been recruited to, within which they are introduced to the hotel's mission statement, which heavily emphasises the ethos of outstanding customer service. After four weeks, employees are sent on a regional induction programme in another hotel within the group.

As well as recruiting those with the right attitude, anyone with the potential to take on supervisory responsibilities is also particularly sought after. The view within the hotel is not that employees are recruited to a particular position, but to a career. Indeed, the hotel group has recently established a 'Career Tracks' programme, which details structured career paths. Thus, staff who demonstrate potential and a willingness to take on greater responsibility are made aware of the promotion opportunities available to them, not just within their own department or hotel but within the hotel group as a whole. Indeed, there is a policy within the group that all positions have to be advertised internally and all internal candidates have to be interviewed. It is only if there is no suitable candidate from within the organisation that external recruitment takes place.

Reflecting the career development ethos within the hotel, training activities focus as heavily on developmental training as on foundation and technical training. Developmental training is offered to staff after they have worked within the organisation for at least eight months to one year. There is no policy specifying the amount of time to be spent in training, but training is nevertheless seen as critical. A 'Training Steps' document, emphasising the cumulative rather than ad-hoc nature of training has been recently introduced. Prior to the commencement of a training programme, staff attend a 'pre-course brief' with their head of department to discuss the relevance and objectives of the course. On returning from the training programme, staff meet again with their head of department for a 'post-course brief' to discuss what they learned from the course, whether it met their expectations and how they will be able to apply the skills they have learned. There is considerable enthusiasm amongst the staff for the training provided. Indeed, the heavy emphasis on training is, in the opinion of the personnel manager, one of the major attractions to the hotel for new staff, and a major factor in encouraging staff retention. Performance appraisals, undertaken every six months, have been introduced recently. These enable staff with the potential to move into supervisory positions to be identified and developed. They also ensure that staff have the requisite confidence, skills and abilities to operate effectively within their current position.

Communication is also heavily emphasised within the hotel. Several formal channels of communication are used to reinforce the company's values, and to provide a two-way forum within which new ideas can be voiced. Issues such as health and safety, technical training and operational aspects of the job are discussed at monthly departmental communication meetings. As a result of initiatives emanating from these meetings, a staff newspaper has been set up, as has a 'green' committee, which looks at ways in which the hotel's operations can be made more environmentally friendly. The billing and ledgering system was also changed following suggestions raised by employees within communication meeting discussions. The company also operates a staff survey, the aim of which is to elicit opinions on a range of issues relating to training, welfare and the level of communication, for example.

As with the other 'HRM' hotels, attempts have been made to empower front-line staff. This is demonstrated by the manner in which complaints are handled. Where staff are faced with a problem they feel they can deal with, they are encouraged to take the initiative rather than to call in a manager. This extends to making reductions to bills where a service, in the judgement of the employee, has not been adequately provided. The hotel's 'Value Policy' states that if a service is not delivered, or if a problem is not remedied, then it should not be charged for. The 'Value Policy' also provides staff with guidelines in terms of making decisions over bill reductions and how much they can discount. However, where major complaints are concerned, staff are encouraged to refer the complaint to the duty manager, on the principle that the customer would feel that their complaint is being taken more seriously if it is dealt with at managerial level.

Although attempts have been made to decentralise authority, and there is heavy emphasis on training and the communication of values to ensure standards of service, there is nevertheless a considerable amount of monitoring and staff surveillance. The hotel is assessed monthly by a mystery customer, who evaluates booking procedures, service delivery, the product, and 'take out' (a subjective assessment of the overall experience). Each department is given a separate score, and shortcomings are indicated. Staff are also routinely monitored by managers in the performance of their day-to-day job tasks to assess whether they meet required standards. These mechanisms are seen as critical in ensuring staff achieve the requisite level of service quality.

Despite the apparent emphasis on formal systems of monitoring and surveillance, there is nevertheless a great deal to suggest that this hotel is operating a wide range of practices commonly associated with an HRM approach. The follow-up interview therefore provides further support for the HRM categorisation adopted within the previous chapter.

Summary

The six follow-up interviews provide support for both the business strategy and the HRM categorisations used in the previous chapter. Looking at the hotels originally categorised as 'other', in the follow-up interviews, both emphasised the importance of service quality. If representative of the hotels classified as 'other' within the previous chapter, the suggestion is that a service quality focus is perceived as the key to competitive success in all but 23 per cent of the hotels within the sample. However, it must be remembered that neither of the hotels in the follow-up interview programme explicitly emphasised cost reduction or price as a key focus, so this conclusion should be treated with caution. There may be considerably greater variation within the business strategies of the hotels within this category than is revealed by the follow-up interviews.

Concerning the 'HRM' and 'non-HRM' categorisations, only one of the six hotels did not fit its classification as a 'non-HRM' hotel. On the whole, the hotels are operating in a manner consistent with their questionnaire responses. The only exception to this concerns single status, whereby none of the hotels visited have completely harmonised terms and conditions of employment, whereas five of the case-study hotels claim to have done so within the questionnaire. Nevertheless, the follow-up interviews validate the questionnaire responses in relation to job design initiatives, the use of performance appraisals, selection tests, training and communication techniques. There is no evidence, as found by Hales (1987), that respondents had in any way misinterpreted the questions asked about or were applying the techniques only to management. The follow-up interviews therefore support the argument presented in Chapter 3 concerning to the extent to which there has been experimentation with new approaches to HRM within the hotel industry.

Investors in People

A further unexpected finding within the follow-up interviews was that five of the six hotels within the sample had Investors in People accreditation. Requiring the fulfilment of set criteria concerning developmental training, communication and the evaluation of the impact of training, Investors in People is seen as the hallmark of a quality employer. The first hotels to have achieved accreditation did so following local-level initiatives. Following these successes, regional offices have increasingly taken up responsibility for Investors in People, with a view to achieving group-wide accreditation. Indeed, in one instance, moves were under way to transfer Investors in People to the group's continental operations.

The sheer number of hotels that are now attempting to gain Investors in People accreditation can be taken as indicative of the importance attached to the manner in which human resources are managed within the industry. While the first hotel within which follow-up interviews were conducted did not receive accreditation until 1993, there were at the time of writing, according to figures from the Investors in People database, 587 hotels seeking accreditation, with 446 having already achieved it. Only a few years ago, Investors in People accreditation would have been virtually unheard of within the industry. However, one interviewee estimated that up to 60 per cent of hotels of the nature under investigation within this analysis in the London area are now either aiming for it or already have it.

The hotels within the follow-up interview programme have engaged in a considerable overhaul of their HRM policies and practices as a result of the process of gaining Investors in People accreditation, particularly in relation to communication and the development of more systematic training and appraisal mechanisms. As one personnel manager commented:

> …going for Investors in People really highlighted the areas where we were doing well with our staff and the areas where we were failing our staff…

Training provision tended to be adequate in terms of the amount of training, but it tended to be too remote from daily job functioning, with staff not being made aware as to why they were being sent on a particular course, or how they could use the skills once they returned. Investors in People led to the realisation that training activity was never evaluated, nor was it linked to the achievement of specific business objectives. As such, a greater focus on the evaluation of the impact of training activity, in terms of its costs and benefits and its effect on the bottom line, has been encouraged. As one personnel manager commented:

> …you become much more focused in terms of your training and develop-ment, in terms of linking it into your business goals, whereas before we just trained and developed because that was what we thought we should be doing…

Investors in People has also led to the realisation that training should be the responsibility of line as well as personnel managers. Line managers were reported to have become increasingly involved in the training process, some-times initiating their own training programmes.

In addition, improvements have been made to communication systems as a result of Investors in People. In the process of going for accreditation, one hotel conducted three monthly surveys of staff to evaluate whether information from senior management was reaching operative grades, only to find out that it sometimes took as long as 12 months for information to filter through. Another hotel found considerable discrepancies in the quality of commu-nication in different areas of the hotel. Some were communicating well because of the nature of the particular head of department. However, information would often be passed down as far as head of department level, and would stop there. To improve on this situation the hotel introduced 'one-to-one' meetings every three months, and increased the frequency of departmental communication meetings to one per month. Attitudes towards the dissemination of information changed considerably, the personnel manager commenting:

> …we are much more open with information than we were before. That was one of our biggest failings…

As a result of the difficulty of separating out the impact of Investors in People from other simultaneously occurring changes, and also because it has in general been introduced in line with the upswing in the business cycle, it is difficult to separate out tangible evidence of its impact on the bottom line. However, one respondent expressed the hope that Investors in People accreditation would raise the profile of the industry, by helping to dispel the image that hotels are poor employers, and by helping to dispel the historical myth that '…anybody can work in a hotel…'.

Influences on HRM decision-making

While the follow-up interviews provide verification of the business strategy and HRM classifications used in the previous chapter, they also allow for a further investigation of the factors that influence management decision-making in relation to HRM policy choice. The previous chapter suggested that chain hotels are more likely to have adopted HRM, while market instability, resistance to change, labour turnover and unionisation have no impact. The next section assesses the importance attached to these influences within the follow-up interview programme.

Hotel chains

The follow-up interviews support the notion that the adoption of HRM is more widespread within hotel chains. However, it would seem that the impact of the head office on the approach taken to HRM at unit level depends a great deal upon the size of the chain. For example, the 'non-HRM cost reducer' is part of a small chain of 13 hotels, and there are only two operational grades above that of general manager. The result is little hierarchy, and little instruction from above in terms of policies and practices. The unit-level personnel manager is therefore free to introduce practices as she sees fit, yet has no guidance or instruction from above in terms of the introduction of new practices.

However, amongst the larger chains, there is considerable evidence of practices developed at regional or head office level being fed down to unit level. The role of the personnel manager is to tailor the policy to their specific situation. The follow-up interviews therefore support the conclusion reached in the previous chapter that innovation emanates primarily from head office, unit-level personnel management rarely initiating innovation. Nevertheless, unit-level personnel is increasingly viewed in a professional light, one respondent commenting that a unit-level personnel manager would not now be appointed within their chain unless they were IPD qualified. In addition, there were examples of individual unit-level managers playing a role in the innovation process. Two respondents described how practices developed at unit level were disseminated through the group via regular meetings of unit-level personnel managers, at which 'best practice' innovations could be discussed. Being part of a large chain therefore facilitated the bottom-up dissemination of locally developed 'best practice'.

Attitudes towards unions

The analysis within the previous chapter suggested that the weak unionisation that exists within the industry has little or no effect on the approach taken to HRM. While it is not possible to test the impact of strong unionisation in the industry, the respondents speculated that the presence of strong unions would undoubtedly slow down the decision-making process and the implementation of new practices, particularly practices that relied upon the ability to communicate directly with the workforce. One respondent who had moved into the industry from a manufacturing environment felt that the non-union nature of the hotel industry was a particularly important factor explaining the relatively higher levels of innovation in terms of HRM within the hotel industry.

However, whereas there is an appreciation of the freedom of action entailed by a lack of strong unions within the industry, there is evidence that managerial prerogative is also used to unilaterally impose unpopular decisions, which in many other industries would be subject to consultation and negotiation. For example, within the 'non-HRM cost reducer', as mentioned earlier, sickness benefit provision was reduced as a cost cutting measure in 1993. The decision to take this action was made without consultation with the workforce. The non-union status of the hotel undoubtedly facilitated this process.

Labour turnover

While the analysis in Chapter 4 suggests that there is no particular relationship between the level of labour turnover and the approach taken to HRM, several questions remain unanswered. Firstly, there is considerable debate relating to the causes of labour turnover within the industry. Secondly, there is considerable debate as to whether turnover should be viewed as problematic – in that it generates higher recruitment and training costs and causes the depletion of valuable firm-specific human capital – or whether it should be seen as a mechanism by which headcount can be reduced and wage costs controlled and by which inefficient staff can be shed. Thirdly, whether labour turnover can be reduced by better management, or whether it should be viewed as a 'fact of life' operational contingency that is unlikely to be affected by HRM-type initiatives, remains open to question. The follow-up interviews conducted here shed light on these debates.

In the event, most respondents viewed labour turnover in a negative light from the point of view of the additional recruitment and training costs generated. Also stressed was the additional pressure put on other staff who have to provide cover for employees who have left, and also the fact that standards are affected, as new members of staff lack hotel-specific knowledge. However, the extent to which turnover is seen as a problem also depends in part on the reason why it is occurring and who is leaving. For example, labour turnover in the 'HRM other' was 48 per cent during 1995. The high proportion of foreign staff on fixed-term contracts boosted this figure. Such staff very often come to the UK with a primary goal of learning English. Hotels in the UK are willing to employ them as they are seen as providing both an international 'flavour' within the hotel, and also an element of flair and creativity acquired on highly-regarded training courses in their home countries. If such workers leave to continue employment in their home countries, labour turnover is seen as an inevitable consequence of choosing to employ foreign workers, and is viewed neither as a problem nor as an indicator of workforce dissatisfaction.

Whether or not labour turnover impacts on the approach taken to HRM is also partly dependent upon the jobs within which quit rates are highest. Within the 'non-HRM other', high rates of turnover amongst kitchen hands is seen as less problematic because these staff do not come into direct contact with the customer, and as such, would not affect the hotel's empowerment programme. This argument calls into question whether HRM in the industry is seen as applying to all workers, or whether it is only applied to certain key groups of workers operating in front-line positions.

However, some respondents suggested that while it is considered problematic, labour turnover is also an inevitable 'fact of life'. The profile of the industry's workforce is quite young, and as such, staff often leave to broaden their horizons. Commenting on the inevitability of labour turnover, the 'non-HRM quality enhancer' interviewee commented

> …a year is a long time in this industry. It's hard work, and people look for a change…

Financial reward is a further reason behind high quit rates. The interviewee within the 'HRM quality enhancer' commented that the buoyancy of the local labour market provided plentiful opportunities for staff to move to boost their salary, either to another hotel or to another industry. The implication therefore is that higher salaries would aid retention. Is paying higher salaries feasible? Not according to the interviewee within the 'non-HRM cost reducer', who commented that the savings in terms of lower recruitment and training costs would not outweigh the additional salary costs, should salaries be increased to a level that would have a significant impact on retention.

This is not to say that labour turnover is unavoidable, or that nothing can be done to reduce it. The training offered to staff is seen as a key factor in encouraging retention at the 'HRM other'. As mentioned earlier, the introduction of multi-skilling and functional flexibility at the 'non-HRM other' is seen to have contributed to a fall in labour turnover. However, in some areas of the hotel, particularly within housekeeping, labour turnover is viewed with a greater degree of inevitability. The 'non-HRM other' has attempted to reduce turnover among chambermaids by giving them responsibility for their own quality standards and hence raising levels of autonomy. So far, the scheme has met with little success, and it is now felt that turnover amongst chambermaids is the result of factors that job design initiatives will do little to solve. Many recruits to housekeeping positions find that the job does not suit child-care arrangements, or that the work is harder than originally anticipated. A number of issues will therefore have to be taken into account if turnover is to be reduced amongst the chambermaids within this hotel.

As can be seen therefore, there is a complex, two-way relationship between approaches taken to HRM and labour turnover. It is seen as a problem, though given the predominance of young workers in the industry, low pay and a high proportion of foreign workers, it is also seen to an extent as inevitable. Nevertheless, HRM initiatives, particularly those relating to training, may prove effective in reducing it. However, as demonstrated by the examples of the chambermaids at the 'non-HRM other', the reduction of labour turnover will remain difficult unless a range of problems leading to employee dissatisfaction can be addressed.

Market instability

It is commonly argued that in instances where demand is seasonal, and where a high proportion of the workforce is employed on temporary contracts, there will be little interest in HRM. However, the previous chapter suggested that for hotels of this nature, seasonality is not a major problem, demand being relatively stable all year round.

The follow-up interviews confirmed this picture. Demand was reported as being stable throughout the year, these being large city-centre hotels reliant only to a very minor extent on holiday trade. Any peaks in demand would indeed be met by the usage of casual labour, though for the most part this would only be necessary on a large scale in conference and banqueting. Daily peaks and troughs faced by all hotel industry operations, for example breakfast shifts, would also be dealt with via the usage of casuals.

Therefore, while seasonality might present an operational problem to hotels reliant on holiday trade, it is not a major issue amongst hotels of the type under investigation here. Being large city-centre hotels with a high proportion of corporate clients, demand is stable. Though trade may dip in August, this can usually be handled by core staff taking holidays and by casuals not being hired. As such, large numbers of temporary seasonal workers are not a necessity within hotels of this nature.

Resistance to change

The analysis in the previous chapter suggests that workforce resistance to change within the hotel industry is low, though resistance to organisational change was seen to be somewhat higher than resistance to technical change. The last chapter also demonstrated that the low level of resistance that does exist has no impact on the approach taken to HRM.

This picture was supported in the main by the follow-up interviews. Typical technical changes included the computerisation of the food and beverage function, front office functions, reservations and housekeeping. Organisational changes included the flattening of structures (for example, the removal of assistant head of department grades), or the merging of functions (for example, bar and restaurant functions). In many respects, the impact of these changes has been greater on the job roles of managers, and reflecting this, resistance to organisational change has tended to be higher amongst management than amongst operative grades. However, management resistance has not been caused by a fear of job loss, as headcount reductions, where necessary, have tended to be handled by natural wastage rather than by redundancies. Fears relating to an expansion of job scope and an increase in responsibilities have created greater problems. For example, in the case of the 'non-HRM other', de-layering did not necessarily result in an increase in the workload of individual managers as it was expected that a more delegative approach to management would develop. However, management anxiety resulted from the fact that they were now responsible for the supervision of a larger team and were responsible for a larger part of the hotel's operations. In turn, this meant they would have to learn how to delegate more effectively, and they would have to develop a greater business awareness of the running of their part of the hotel. This anxiety was eventually addressed through management training initiatives focusing on the development of team leadership skills, interpersonal skills and business skills via business simulation exercises.

Where operative-level staff are concerned, there has been an apparent willingness to embrace change. Staff responses to computerisation were reported as positive. Similarly, as stated by the interviewee within the 'non-HRM other', staff viewed multi-skilling favourably, as it increased their skill range, and generally added variety to jobs.

Conclusions and discussion

The follow-up interviews confirm the validity of both the business strategy categorisation and the HRM/non-HRM categorisation used within the previous chapter. Concerning the business strategy categorisation, hotels categorised as 'quality enhancers' and 'cost reducers' seem to be correctly classified, although attitudes towards the importance of cost reduction and price competition have changed in one of the 'cost reducers' since the time the questionnaire was undertaken. Both of the hotels classified as 'other' display similar approaches to those categorised as 'quality enhancers'. This would suggest that quality enhancement is seen as the key to competitive success in all but 23 per cent of the hotels within the sample. However, as mentioned earlier, this inference remains somewhat speculative, and there may be much more diversity amongst the hotels within the 'other' category than is revealed by the analysis of the two hotels under consideration here.

The follow-up interviews also demonstrate the validity of the 'HRM/non-HRM' categorisation used within the previous chapter. All three of the 'HRM' hotels displayed characteristics commonly associated with an HRM approach.

Only one of the 'non-HRM' hotels was incorrectly classified, that being the 'non-HRM other', which in the event, had adopted a wider range of HRM practices than suggested within the survey response.

Equally importantly, the follow-up interviews also provide corroborating evidence for the results reported in Chapter 3, concerning the extent to which HRM has been adopted within the hotel industry. The 'HRM hotels' within which follow-up interviews were carried out have introduced a wide range of practices commonly associated with an HRM approach. There was no evidence that the practices asked about in the questionnaire had been misinterpreted, or that they were being used for the purposes of labour intensification, as found by Hales (1987). The follow-up interviews therefore strongly endorse the conclusions reached within Chapter 3, and suggest that there is considerable substance behind the widespread adoption of the rhetoric of HRM within the hotel industry.

Note

1   The negative response to the question concerning the realistic use of job previews, despite the fact that such practices were clearly in place, may further explain the classification of this hotel as 'non-HRM'.

6 HRM and performance in the hotel industry[1]

The analyses conducted within Chapters 3 and 5 have demonstrated an undeniably high degree of experimentation with new approaches to HRM within the hotels under investigation here. This chapter returns to the 1995 Survey of Human Resource Management in the Hotel Industry in order to examine the relationship between HRM, business strategy and organisational effectiveness. Effectiveness is considered in terms of human resource outcomes such as commitment, flexibility and absenteeism, and also in terms of performance outcomes such as quality of service and financial performance. This is an important test of the relevance of HRM within the hotel industry. It would only be sensible to encourage the adoption of such an approach if it can be demonstrated that it has a beneficial impact on performance.

The analysis of the relationship between HRM and performance has become a research key issue in recent times. Researchers have used large-scale data sets to attempt to ascertain the links between what Wood and Albanese (1995) and Wood and De Menezes (1998) describe as high commitment management (HRM), or what Huselid (1995) describes as 'high-performance work practices', and performance. However, as discussed in Chapter 1, researchers have tended for the most part, to either focus on manufacturing (for example Arthur (1994) looked at steel minimills and MacDuffie (1995) focused on the auto industry), or alternatively, they have not treated services as a variable, but have looked at the HRM and performance relationship across the economy as a whole (see, for example, Fernie and Metcalf, 1995; Huselid, 1995). With systematic tests of the relationship between HRM and performance yet to be conducted within the services, it would seem that the tendency for the services to be overlooked in HRM and industrial relations research is now being replicated within the debate concerning the impact of HRM on performance. By looking at the HRM and performance relationship within a service-related context, the analysis reported here begins to redress this imbalance.

Hypothesis to be tested

Typical analyses of HRM and performance have, in the main, focused on two key concepts – internal and external fit. These concepts will form the basis of the analysis to be undertaken here.

Tests of external fit

The situational contingency models presented by Kochan and Barocci (1985), Miles and Snow (1984), Schuler and Jackson (1987) and Tichy, Fombrun and Devanna (1982) suggest that the appropriateness, or effectiveness of HRM will vary depending on organisational lifecycle or the product market within which the organisation is operating. For example, Schuler and Jackson (1987) and Schuler (1989) argue that HRM will only prove effective if the firm emphasises the importance of either quality enhancement or innovation within its business strategy. If the organisation is competing on price, the logical HR approach would be a focus on numerical flexibility and wage cost control. In such a situation, the values and goals imbued within HRM would be inconsistent with the organisation's primary cost-reduction goals. External fit therefore refers to the 'organisational logic' argument that HR strategy should be meshed with business strategy, such that there is a consistency between the values and aims within each (MacDuffie, 1995: 199).

The few attempts that have been made to assess the importance of external fit have failed to find evidence that the impact of HRM is contingent upon the approach taken to business strategy. Nevertheless, researchers have remained reluctant to write off the concept. For example, Huselid (1995: 667) describes the conceptual arguments relating to external fit as 'compelling'. Becker and Gerhart (1996) argue that the universal effects demonstrated within much of the research do not necessarily contradict the importance of contingency effects. They argue that results demonstrating universality operate on the level of 'architecture'. Hence, the same practice – merit pay for example – may be equally applicable in firms with differing business strategies, but the behaviours rewarded within the merit pay system will differ depending on approach taken to business strategy. As such, these results do not preclude the possibility that performance is contingent upon the tailoring of practices to firm-specific situations.

The first issue to be addressed within this analysis is therefore whether, within the hotel industry, the effectiveness of HRM is contingent upon the approach to business strategy that has been adopted.

Is HRM universally relevant within the hotel industry?

While it might be the case that the effectiveness of HRM is dependent upon it being coupled with a quality enhancer business strategy, is there any evidence that an 'HRM quality enhancer' approach is likely to prove the most effective within the context of the hotel industry? This is an important issue when considering the universal relevance of HRM.

When testing universalism, it is important to acknowledge the difference between the universal effects that HRM might have, and the universal relevance of HRM as an approach. Where universal effects are concerned, the implication is that, contrary to external fit arguments, HRM has performance effects irrespective of circumstances, or irrespective of the business strategy adopted. Most tests of universalism have focused on this issue.

By contrast, tests of the universal relevance of HRM do not contradict contingency arguments. It might be the case that the effectiveness of HRM is contingent upon a coupling with a quality enhancer or innovator strategy (supporting the 'organisational logic' contingency argument discussed earlier). However, if all hotels are experiencing greater product market turbulence and are increasingly under pressure to adopt a business strategy emphasising flexibility, quality and innovation, the implication is that an HRM approach will be universally relevant. This would not detract from the contingency argument that the success of HRM is dependent upon it being coupled with a particular approach to business strategy.

Whether HRM has universal relevance therefore depends to a large part upon the nature of the industry product market. For example, Guest (1987) and Walton (1985) suggest that, to varying degrees, all organisations are operating in increasingly uncertain environments, within which the emphasis is on responsiveness to customer needs and on the provision of higher quality, customised goods and services. In such conditions, innovative or developmental approaches to HRM, aimed at eliciting employee flexibility, adaptability and commitment to the organisation, will have a universal relevance.

However, if an industry product market is more diverse in nature than is suggested by Guest (1987) and Walton (1985), there is no reason why HRM should necessarily prove effective. It may be the case that in certain situations, cost control or price competition remains important, and that an HR strategy focusing on cost reduction, numerical flexibility and a careful control over headcount will prove more effective. If this can be shown to be the case, support for the universal relevance of HRM is lost. The second aim of this chapter is to test this issue.

Is internal fit important?

The second notion of fit that HRM researchers have explored relates to internal fit. This refers to the synergistic benefits resulting from the introduction of HRM as an institutionally supported package of practices that cohere and mutually reinforce each other.

Varying degrees of support for a relationship between fit of this nature and performance has been found within empirical analyses to date (see for example Guest and Hoque, 1994b; Huselid, 1995; Ichniowski, Shaw and Prennushi, 1994; MacDuffie, 1995). The third aim of this chapter is to test whether hotels claiming to have introduced HRM techniques within an institutionally supported, coherent package, outperform those that have introduced similar HRM practices, though in an *ad hoc* fashion and not as part of an overarching policy or strategy.

The data

The data used here are taken from the 1995 Survey of Human Resource Management in the Hotel Industry. When missing data are accounted for, and when establishments with fewer than 25 employees are dropped, 209 hotels in total are used within the analysis.

Dependent variables

Within the 1995 survey, data were collected on a wide range of both HR outcome and performance outcome measures, against which the effectiveness of HRM is commonly assessed.

HR outcomes

Respondents were asked to rate each of the HR outcomes asked about within their own hotels on a scale of one (very low) to five (very high). The HR outcomes asked about were as follows:

i)   The commitment to the organisation of lower grades of staff.
ii) The level of job satisfaction of lower grades of staff.
iii) The flexibility of staff.
iv) The ability of staff to move between jobs as the work demands.
v)   The quality of work of lower grades of staff.
vi) The quality of staff currently employed.

Respondents were also asked to provide information relating to the number of days lost through all types of absence during 1994. The average absenteeism rate for 1994 was 8.35 per cent.

Respondents were also asked whether or not there had been an industrial dispute at the hotel within the last six years. This variable is not used in the analysis as the incidence of industrial disputes is so low, with only four hotels in the total sample of 209 having experienced any industrial action during the six years prior to the survey being undertaken.

Performance outcomes

Three questions were asked concerning performance outcomes. Respondents were asked to rate each on a scale of one (much worse) to five (much better). These questions were as follows:

i)   How well does labour productivity at your hotel compare with the hotel industry average?
ii)   How does quality of service at your hotel compare with the hotel industry average?
iii) How would you compare the financial performance of your hotel with the hotel industry average?

Independent variables

The measures of HRM to be used to test the relationship between HRM and the performance measures outlined above are based upon the 22 HRM practices listed within Table 3.4 in Chapter 3. These practices relate to terms and conditions of employment, recruitment and selection, training, job design, communication, consultation, quality issues and pay systems. The mean number of practices used within the sample used here is 13.4. The precise manner in which the HRM independent variables are constructed to test the impact of internal and external fit, and the universal relevance of HRM, is discussed in detail within the following sections.

Testing the impact of external fit

As suggested by Schuler and Jackson (1987), HRM should only prove effective within hotels emphasising a quality enhancer or innovator approach to business strategy, and should prove ineffective where the hotel's business strategy emphasises cost cutting, or competition on price factors.

To test this hypothesis, the business strategy typology introduced in Chapter 4, which draws on the analysis presented by Schuler and Jackson (1987), is used here. The first category consists of hotels with a competitive strategy focusing on cost reduction or price competition. The second category consists of hotels with a competitive strategy focusing on quality enhancement. The third category consists of hotels with an ambiguous approach to business strategy. Forty-seven, or 22.49 per cent of the hotels within the sample fall into the cost reducer category; 104, or 49.76 per cent of the sample fall into the quality enhancer category; and 58, or 27.75 per cent of the sample fall, into the 'other' category.

The development of a hypothesis concerning the relationship between the adoption of HRM and performance is somewhat more difficult where the 'other' hotels are concerned than where the cost reducer or quality enhancer hotels are concerned. The ambiguity implied within the business strategies of the 'other' hotels suggests they may be what Porter (1985: 16–17) describes as 'stuck in the middle'.

However, a focus on quality does not necessarily preclude a simultaneous focus on costs. Indeed, as Porter (1985) argues, firms focusing on quality should attempt to minimise costs as far as possible so long as cost reduction is not detrimental to the achievement of the firm's primary quality enhancement focus (and vice versa). Therefore, if the hotels within the 'other' category have a primary focus on quality enhancement, a relationship between the adoption of HRM and performance might be expected. Less of a relationship might be expected if these hotels are focusing primarily on cost reduction. Nothing more is known about the nature of the business strategy within the 'other' hotels. Thus, if business strategy has a moderating effect, a relationship between HRM and performance amongst the 'other' category could be taken as indicative that these hotels are indeed focusing primarily on quality enhancement.

The measure of HRM to be used within this part of the analysis is cumulative, with each hotel being ranked according to the extent to which they have adopted the twenty-two HRM practices discussed earlier. The aim of this variable is to examine the relationship between the extent to which HRM practices have been adopted and performance. By splitting the sample as described above, and then regressing this cumulative HRM variable on each of the dependent outcome variables, it will be possible to assess the effectiveness of HRM in the context of 'cost reducer', 'quality enhancer' and 'other' business strategies.

Testing the universal relevance of HRM

Is it the case that the hotels within the sample adopting HRM coupled with quality enhancement enjoy performance levels superior to those achieved by other hotels? Answers to this question will shed light on whether HRM holds universal relevance within the industry.

This issue is tested as follows. The sample, having been split three ways to perform the external fit tests described above, is re-classified here to enable comparisons between business strategy categories as follows:

1) 'Low-HRM cost reducers' using 10 or fewer HR practices. Ten hotels fall into this category.
2) 'Medium-HRM cost reducers' using more than 10 but less than 16 HR practices. Twenty-seven hotels fall into this category.
3) 'High-HRM cost reducers' using 16 or more HR practices. Ten hotels fall into this category.
4) 'Low-HRM quality enhancers' using 10 or less HR practices. Twenty-two hotels fall into this category.
5) 'Medium-HRM quality enhancers' using more than 10 but less than 16 HR practices. Forty-five hotels fall into this category.
6) 'High-HRM quality enhancers' using 16 or more HR practices. Thirty-seven hotels fall into this category.
7) 'Low-HRM others' using 10 or less HR practices. Thirteen hotels fall into this category.
8) 'Medium-HRM others' using more than 10 but less than 16 HR practices. Twenty-two hotels fall into this category.
9) 'High-HRM others' using 16 or more HR practices. Twenty-three hotels fall into this category.

This series of dummies enables a comparative analysis of the level of performance dependent on the approach taken to HRM and to business strategy. Holding category six constant will show whether 'high-HRM quality enhancer' hotels outperform the other categories of hotel within the sample.

Testing the importance of internal fit

The final hypothesis to be tested concerns the importance of introducing HRM as a synergistic package of mutually supporting practices. Of the hotels adopting a wide range of HRM practices, those introducing their HRM practices as a coherent, institutionally supported synergistic package should outperform hotels within which HRM has been introduced in a more *ad hoc* manner.

In order to test this issue, a trichotomous variable is constructed as follows:[2]

i) 'Strategic HRM' hotels: above average (14 or more) usage of HRM practices strategically integrated with each other. Seventy-one hotels (43.83 per cent) fall into this category.

ii) 'Non-strategic HRM' hotels: above average (14 or more) usage of HRM practices, which are not strategically integrated. Twenty-five hotels (15.43 per cent) fall into this category.

iii) 'Low-HRM' hotels: below average (less than 14) usage of HRM practices. Sixty-six hotels (40.74 per cent) fall into this category.

A hotel has 'strategically integrated' its HRM practices in the typology above if the respondent claims firstly that the hotel has a human resource strategy, formally endorsed and actively supported by the top management at the hotel, and secondly that HR policies are deliberately integrated with each other. If internal fit is important, the 'strategic HRM' hotels within the first of these dummies should outperform the other hotels within the sample.

Control variables

The following control variables are included within the analysis. The first is a dichotomous variable concerning union presence. This variable simply concerns whether or not a union is present, irrespective of whether it is recognised. The second concerns establishment size, with dummies for hotels with between 50–99 employees, 99–199 employees and 200 or more employees being included within the regressions (the omitted category being hotels with between 25–49 employees). The third concerns whether or not hotels are UK or foreign owned. The fourth concerns the price of a standard room per night. The fifth concerns the age of the hotel.

Results

How important is external fit?

Looking firstly at HR outcomes, Table 6.1 demonstrates a strong link between the cumulative HRM variable and all of the HR outcome measures for the sample as a whole, with the exception of labour turnover. Concerning the

Table 6.1 The relationship between HRM and human resource outcomes in the hotel industry

	All hotels	Cost reducers	Quality enhancers	Others
Organisational commitment				
HRM	.095 (.021)***	.127 (.055)**	.107 (.032)***	.103 (.04)**
Union presence	.016 (.243)	−.318 (.838)	−.164 (.311)	.459 (.505)
50–99 employees	.101 (.273)	.058 (.507)	.342 (.421)	−.1 (.629)
100–199 employees	−.163 (.281)	.275 (.543)	.044 (.408)	−.829 (.675)
200+ employees	.251 (.345)	.103 (.615)	.661 (.51)	.231 (.827)
Foreign owned	.305 (.245)	−.321 (.659)	.417 (.331)	.525 (.486)
Age	.004 (.006)	−.021 (.017)	.014 (.008)*	.002 (.011)
Price	−.002 (.003)	−.004 (.006)	−.002 (.004)	−.003 (.005)
n	209	47	104	58
R^2	.055	.069	.086	.091
Job satisfaction				
HRM	.12 (.024)***	.151 (.063)**	.129 (.035)***	.153 (.046)***
Union presence	−.276 (.26)	.097 (1.007)	−.464 (.338)	.374 (.545)
50–99 employees	.466 (.293)	.944 (.577)	.287 (.45)	.35 (.678)
100–199 employees	.237 (.299)	1.201 (.633)*	−.04 (.433)	−.082 (.724)
200+ employees	.384 (.366)	1.38 (.722)*	−.118 (.535)	.933 (.89)
Foreign owned	.188 (.258)	−.302 (.749)	.606 (.351)*	−.471 (.518)
Age	.005 (.006)	−.049 (.02)**	.02 (.009)**	−.007 (.012)
Price	.001 (.003)	−.000 (.007)	.002 (.004)	.002 (.006)
n	208	47	103	58
R^2	.089	.172	.137	.155
Staff flexibility				
HRM	.06 (.021)***	−.013 (.054)	.054 (.031)*	.131 (.045)***
Union presence	−.069 (.243)	1.031 (.915)	−.077 (.308)	−.32 (.531)
50–99 employees	−.26 (.281)	.164 (.52)	−.611 (.441)	−.705 (.726)
100–199 employees	−.497 (.289)*	.096 (.555)	−.734 (.432)*	−1.067 (.773)
200+ employees	−.409 (.352)	−.497 (.628)	−.581 (.525)	−.272 (.916)
Foreign owned	.186 (.249)	1.498 (.721)**	−.187 (.331)	.687 (.541)
Age	.006 (.006)	−.011 (.018)	.023 (.01)**	−.001 (.011)
Price	.000 (.003)	−.009 (.006)	.005 (.004)	−.006 (.006)
n	209	47	104	58
R^2	.029	.098	.056	.129
Ability to move staff between jobs as required				
HRM	.066 (.021)***	.037 (.054)	.076 (.031)**	.082 (.042)**
Union presence	−.167 (.24)	1.788 (1.024)*	−.185 (.305)	−.768 (.526)
50–99 employees	−.382 (.277)	−.619 (.524)	−.692 (.434)	−.355 (.658)
100–199 employees	−.527 (.285)*	.214 (.557)	−.868 (.426)**	−1.148 (.71)
200+ employees	−.426 (.348)	−.791 (.642)	−.636 (.516)	.64 (.879)
Foreign owned	.102 (.246)	.467 (.688)	−.074 (.329)	.607 (.506)
Age	.002 (.006)	−.038 (.018)**	.01 (.008)	.006 (.011)
Price	−.001 (.003)	.000 (.006)	.001 (.004)	−.011 (.006)**
n	208	47	103	58
R^2	.031	.137	.049	.164

Table 6.1 (continued)

	All hotels	Cost reducers	Quality enhancers	Others
Quality of work				
HRM	.082 (.022)***	.079 (.055)	.101 (.034)***	.111 (.046)**
Union presence	−.22 (.254)	−.788 (.865)	−.177 (.329)	−.624 (.616)
50–99 employees	.153 (.286)	.382 (.518)	.273 (.447)	.612 (.849)
100–199 employees	−.104 (.294)	.26 (.556)	−.258 (.432)	.267 (.891)
200+ employees	−.011 (.361)	−.017 (.63)	−.347 (.534)	1.56 (1.062)
Foreign owned	.052 (.256)	−.415 (.675)	.321 (.353)	.111 (.548)
Age.	006 (.006)	.003 (.018)	.013 (.009)	.004 (.012)
Price	.005 (.003)*	−.002 (.006)	.007 (.004)*	.003 (.006)
n	209	47	104	58
R^2	.051	.037	.094	.148
Quality of staff				
HRM	.053 (.021)**	.049 (.054)	.051 (.032)	.099 (.041)**
Union presence	−.044 (.245)	−.552 (.842)	−.389 (.324)	.847 (.526)
50–99 employees	−.027 (.274)	.186 (.508)	−.291 (.436)	.931 (.636)
100–199 employees	.013 (.283)	.269 (.544)	−.147 (.422)	.55 (.676)
200+ employees	−.103 (.347)	−.534 (.619)	−.06 (.521)	1.217 (.853)
Foreign owned	.002 (.246)	−.416 (.654)	.298 (.342)	−.013 (.478)
Age	.012 (.006)*	−.005 (.017)	.022 (.009)**	.015 (.011)
Price	.004 (.003)	−.001 (.006)	.004 (.004)	.003 (.006)
n	209	47	104	58
R^2	.031	.046	.073	.112
Absenteeism				
HRM	.013 (.357)	.102 (.175)	−.077 (.053)	.051 (.052)
Union presence	.388 (.392)	−.843 (1.481)	.628 (.463)	1.441 (.775)*
50–99 employees	−.573 (.396)	−1.076 (.772)	.496 (.574)	−.53 (.763)
100–199 employees	.106 (.436)	−.023 (1.7)	1.033 (.591)*	.442 (.899)
200+ employees	−.054 (.592)	−2.766 (1.853)	2.412 (.871)***	.113 (1.24)
Foreign owned	−.318 (.353)	.522 (1.437)	.628 (.463)	−.979 (.63)
Age	−.005 (.01)	.034 (.041)	−.004 (.011)	−.017 (.022)
Price	.001 (.004)	.011 (.021)	−.013 (.006)**	−.002 (.009)
n	100	18	49	33
R^2	.006	.245	.052	.147

Notes: Ordered probit analysis, except for absenteeism equation (OLS analysis).
Absenteeism dependent variable = Log of $(P/(1-P))$ where P=absenteeism.
R^2 is pseudo except for absenteeism equation (adjusted).
*** significant at 1 per cent, ** significant at 5 per cent, * significant at 10 per cent.
Coefficients given (standard errors in brackets).
HRM variable is cumulative.

'quality enhancer' subsample, as predicted, the strong positive relationship identified within the sample as a whole is replicated, with the exception of only one measure, namely the quality of staff currently employed. The labour turnover variable remains insignificant. Thus, for hotels with a business strategy based on quality enhancement, the extent to which HRM is used is strongly and positively related to most of the HR outcomes under investigation here.

Amongst hotels pursuing cost reducer strategies, Table 6.1 demonstrates a positive correlation between the extent to which HRM is practised and the level of organisational commitment and job satisfaction. However, there is no relationship between the extent to which HRM practices have been adopted and the flexibility, quality or absenteeism measures. HRM would seem therefore to be more effective amongst the quality enhancer hotels than amongst the cost reducer hotels in terms of achieving the HR outcomes under investigation here.

Looking at the 'other' establishments, Table 6.1 demonstrates positive correlations between the cumulative HRM variable and all of the HR outcome measures, again with the exception of absenteeism. The impact of HRM within these hotels would seem to be more akin to the impact of HRM amongst the quality enhancers than amongst the cost reducers.

Thus, amongst the hotels with an identifiable business strategy, there is evidence to suggest that HRM proves more effective in terms of achieving HR outcomes where the business strategy emphasises quality enhancement rather than cost control. These results provide moderate support for the importance of external fit. However, given that HRM also impacts positively on two of the HR outcome variables where the cost reducers are concerned, this conclusion should be treated with caution.

The results concerning the relationship between HRM and performance outcomes provide stronger evidence for the hypothesis that the effectiveness of HRM is dependent upon the achievement of external fit. As shown by Table 6.2, across the sample as a whole, there is a strong positive relationship between the extent to which HRM is used and all three of the organisational performance measures. However, where cost reducer hotels are concerned, this positive relationship completely disappears. It is particularly indicative that the relationship between HRM and financial performance is very slightly negative (though insignificantly so). Overall, as hypothesised, there is absolutely no evidence that the adoption of HRM leads to improved performance where hotels put a premium on cost control within their business strategies.

The converse is true of quality enhancer hotels. The HRM measure correlates strongly with both the quality of service and the financial performance measure. The only performance measure not related to the extent to which

Table 6.2 The relationship between HRM and organisational performance in the hotel industry

	All hotels	Cost reducers	Quality enhancers	Others
Labour productivity				
HRM	.07 (.022)***	.086 (.058)	.046 (.031)	.127 (.044)***
Union presence	−.236 (.245)	−.385 (.877)	−.168 (.306)	−.427 (.522)
50–99 employees	−.65 (.286)**	.06 (.535)	−1.255 (.463)***	−.72 (.672)
100–199 employees	−1.03 (.297)***	−.018 (.575)	−1.51 (.458)***	−1.408(.728)*
200+ employees	−.785 (.358)**	−.806 (.684)	−.948 (.534)*	−1.271 (.914)
Foreign owned	.479 (.251)*	1.109 (.717)	.441 (.334)	.407 (.511)
Age	.009 (.006)	−.006 (.018)	.016 (.008)*	.013 (.011)
Price	.002 (.003)	−.007 (.007)	.002 (.004)	.005 (.006)
n	205	47	101	57
Pseudo R^2	.066	.106	.092	.12
Quality of service				
HRM	.092 (.022)***	.017 (.053)	.128 (.035)***	.077 (.042)*
Union presence	−.266 (.248)	−.338 (.846)	−.19 (.32)	−.436 (.517)
50–99 employees	−.215 (.278)	.525 (.513)	−1.222 (.459)***	.408 (.657)
100–199 employees	.014 (.286)	.388 (.549)	−.626 (.44)	.471 (.697)
200+ employees	.194 (.352)	.136 (.622)	−.495 (.536)	1.191 (.866)
Foreign owned	.228 (.254)	1.038 (.699)	.005 (.352)	.332 (.481)
Age	.001 (.006)	.005 (.018)	.009 (.008)	−.003 (.01)
Price	.01 (.003)***	.008 (.006)	.014 (.004)	.004 (.005)
n	204	47	100	57
Pseudo R^2	.094	.065	.173	.08
Financial performance				
HRM	.072 (.021)***	−.054 (.054)	.086 (.032)***	.103 (.04)***
Union presence	−.35 (.239)	.437 (.835)	−.362 (.306)	−.137 (.492)
50–99 employees	−.057 (.272)	−.269 (.513)	−.367 (.429)	.762 (.612)
100–199 employees	−.358 (.281)	−.29 (.551)	−.562 (.418)	.145 (.652)
200+ employees	.206 (.347)	−.808 (.635)	.385 (.513)	.99 (.853)
Foreign owned	.336 (.252)	1.998 (.808)**	.247 (.34)	.151 (.474)
Age	.001 (.006)	.008 (.017)	.014 (.009)	−.012 (.01)
Price	.007 (.003)***	.006 (.006)	.007 (.004)*	.01 (.005)*
n	204	47	100	57
Pseudo R^2	.067	.087	.116	.109

Notes: Ordered probit analysis. Coefficients given (standard errors in brackets).
 *** significant at 1 per cent, ** significant at 5 per cent, * significant at 10 per cent.
HRM variable is cumulative.

HRM is practised is labour productivity. This may not come as a surprise, since within hotels emphasising service quality above cost control, labour productivity – typically measured as customer–staff ratio – may be seen as less important than the level of customer–staff contact, if the aim is to provide a more 'personal', high quality, attentive service.

Looking at the hotels in the 'other' category, as with the quality enhancer hotels, a strong relationship is in evidence between the extent to which HRM is practised and performance. Thus, once again, it seems that the behaviour of these hotels resembles more strongly that of the quality enhancers than the cost reducers.

The results within this section support the external fit hypothesis that the effectiveness of HRM is strongly dependent upon congruence with business strategy. A positive correlation between the cumulative HRM variable and effectiveness only exists within quality enhancer and 'other' hotels. Where hotels emphasise cost control, there is no relationship whatsoever between HRM and quality of service, productivity and possibly most importantly, financial performance.

The universal relevance of HRM

The aim of this part of the analysis is to assess whether the hotels adopting a 'high-HRM quality enhancer' approach are the highest performing hotels within the sample. Such a finding would suggest that HRM coupled with quality enhancement holds universal relevance within the hotel industry, with hotels focusing on cost reduction or a low-HRM approach achieving sub-optimal performance. By contrast, if 'low-HRM cost reducer' hotels are performing equally effectively, the implication will be that a high-HRM approach is not necessarily universally relevant, and that there is sufficient diversity within the industry product market for alternative approaches to business strategy and HRM to prove equally effective.

The results in Table 6.3 would seem to indicate that in relation to HR outcomes, the hotels adopting a quality enhancer approach to business strategy in conjunction with a 'high-HRM' approach are indeed performing best. These hotels are not outperformed on any of the HR outcome measures asked about. In relation to quality of work, the 'high-HRM quality enhancers' outperform all the other categories of hotels. They outperform five of the other eight categories in relation to organisational commitment and job satisfaction, and four of the other eight in relation to staff flexibility and the ability to move staff as the work demands. In addition, absenteeism is lower within the 'high-

Table 6.3 HRM, strategy and human resource outcomes in the hotel industry

	Organisational commitment	Quality of work	Job satisfaction	Flexibility of staff	Quality of staff	Ability to move staff	Absence rate
'Low-HRM cost reducers'	-1.358 (.422)***	-1.537 (.451)***	-.997 (.449)**	-.546 (.419)	-.884 (.417)**	-1.265 (.417)***	.56 (.819)
'Medium-HRM cost reducers'	-.529 (.291)*	-.618 (.31)**	-.478 (.31)	-.576 (.296)*	-.347 (.297)	-.705 (.292)**	.763 (.464)
'High-HRM cost reducers'	-.013 (.404)	-1.087 (.439)**	-.099 (.429)	-.336 (.41)	-.861 (.414)**	-.168 (.405)	1.843 (1.015)*
'Low-HRM quality enhancers'	-1.215 (.314)***	-1.143 (.334)***	-1.242 (.334)***	-.594 (.311)*	-.486 (.315)	-.948 (.312)***	.636 (.625)
'Medium-HRM quality enhancers'	-.326 (.254)	-.652 (.275)**	-.646 (.273)**	-.404 (.26)	-.204 (.261)	-.171 (.255)	.503 (.409)
'Low-HRM others'	-.966 (.376)***	-1.513 (.408) ***	-.962 (.407)**	-.823 (.376)**	-1.38 (.383)***	-.973 (.375)***	.004 (.56)
'Medium-HRM others'	-1.035 (.316)***	-1.289 (.342)***	-1.152 (.341)***	-.568 (.316)*	-.924 (.32)***	-.406 (.312)	.108 (.471)
'High-HRM others'	-.177 (.305)	-.726 (.329)**	.189 (.323)	.17 (.317)	-.37 (.312)	-.158 (.305)	.601 (.461)
Foreign owned	.368 (.257)	.23 (.265)	.368 (.275)	.266 (.261)	.131 (.252)	-.022 (.25)	-.417 (.389)
Union presence	-.191 (.256)	-.413 (.272)	-.459 (.276)*	-.214 (.257)	-.104 (.26)	-.309 (.254)	.05 (.438)
50-99 employees	.216 (.283)	.269 (.3)	.63 (.307)**	-.323 (.292)	-.001 (.285)	-.407 (.287)	-.474 (.436)
100-199 employees	-.105 (.286)	-.141 (.304)	.366 (.307)	-.54 (.296)*	-.053 (.29)	-.537 (.292)*	.191 (.482)
200+ employees	.258 (.359)	-.053 (.38)	.392 (.382)	-.412 (.366)	-.089 (.363)	-.562 (.363)	-.026 (.665)
Age	.004 (.006)	.01 (.007)	.006 (.006)	.006 (.006)	.015 (.007)**	-.003 (.006)	-.009 (.011)
Price	-.002 (.003)	.006 (.003)*	.001 (.003)	-.000 (.003)	.005 (.003)*	-.003 (.003)	-.002 (.005)
n	209	209	208	209	209	208	100
Pseudo R^2	.087	.12	.123	.053	.078	.062	-.002

Notes: Ordered probit analysis except for absence equation (OLS analysis).
Absenteeism dependent variable = Log of $(P/(1-P))$ where P=absenteeism.
Coefficients given (standard errors in brackets).
All regressions control for region.
*** significant at 1 per cent, ** significant at 5 per cent, * significant at 10 per cent.
Omitted category = 'High-HRM quality enhancers'.

HRM quality enhancers' than within the 'high-HRM cost reducers'. The evidence therefore suggests that a high-HRM approach, where it is coupled with a quality enhancer approach to business strategy, leads to superior HR outcomes within the hotel industry.

The results in Table 6.4 further suggest that the 'high-HRM quality enhancers' are the highest performing hotels within the sample. They perform significantly better than all categories of firms on at least one of the organisational performance measures used, with the exception of 'high-HRM other' hotels. The evidence therefore suggests that a focus on cost reduction or on price factors leads to sub-optimal performance within the industry.

The results here therefore support the contention that a 'high-HRM quality enhancer' approach is universally relevant to hotels within the sector of the industry under investigation in this analysis. There would seem to be no real scope for alternative approaches based around cost reduction to achieve comparable performance results.

Table 6.4 HRM, strategy and performance outcomes in the hotel industry

	Labour productivity	Quality of service	Financial performance
'Low-HRM cost reducers'	−.916 (.427)**	−.798 (.415)*	−.38 (.419)
'Medium-HRM cost reducers'	−.421 (.296)	−.829 (.301)***	−.451 (.296)
'High-HRM cost reducers'	−.322 (.413)	−.399 (.411)	−.673 (.404)*
'Low-HRM quality enhancers'	−.509 (.324)	−1.079 (.333)***	−.879 (.325)***
'Medium-HRM quality enhancers'	−.265 (.258)	−.26 (.264)	−.713 (.261)***
'Low-HRM others'	−.953 (.381)**	−.991 (.4)**	−1.207 (.383)***
'Medium-HRM others'	−.405 (.324)	−.601 (.323)*	−.421 (.321)
'High-HRM others'	.098 (.31)	−.145 (.311)	−.089 (.308)
Foreign owned	.443 (.253)*	.37 (.261)	.413 (.267)
Union presence	−.288 (.258)	−.375 (.262)	−.231 (.254)
50–99 employees	−.721 (.296)**	−.147 (.288)	.004 (.284)
100–199 employees	−1.093 (.302)***	.082 (.293)	−.241 (.289)
200+ employees	−.882 (.373)**	.398 (.366)	.242 (.363)
Age	.008 (.006)	.004 (.006)	.003 (.006)
Price	−.000 (.003)	.013 (.003)***	.006 (.003)*
n	205	204	204
Pseudo R^2	.087	.12	.116

Notes: Ordered probit analysis. Coefficients given (standard errors in brackets).
All regressions control for region.
*** significant at 1 per cent, ** significant at 5 per cent, * significant at 10 per cent.
Omitted category = 'high-HRM quality enhancers'.

Table 6.5 HRM, internal fit and human resource outcomes in the hotel industry

	Organisational commitment	Job satisfaction	Staff flexibility	Ability to move staff between jobs	Quality of work	Quality of staff	Absence rate
'Strategic HRM'	.711 (.2)***	.896 (.215)**	.39 (.198)**	.491 (.198)**	.824 (.216)***	.629 (.205)***	.103 (.304)
'Non-strategic HRM'	.528 (.266)**	.436 (.281)	.38 (.269)	.353 (.266)	-.036 (.282)	.341 (.272)	.135 (.408)
Union presence	.104 (.264)	-.128 (.279)	-.142 (.263)	-.284 (.261)	-.072 (.279)	.013 (.269)	.452 (.411)
50–99 employees	.202 (.335)	.337 (.357)	-.41 (.348)	-.47 (.344)	.2 (.359)	-.057 (.34)	-.012 (.473)
100–199 employees	-.116 (.34)	.082 (.36)	-.597 (.355)*	-.763 (.352)**	-.061 (.365)	.041 (.347)	.607 (.507)
200+ employees	.576 (.424)	.277 (.444)	-.346 (.434)	-.199 (.431)	.191 (.45)	.289 (.432)	1.32 (.728)*
Foreign owned	.494 (.268)*	.308 (.279)	.083 (.27)	.136 (.269)	.186 (.284)	.144 (.272)	.022 (.376)
Age	.008 (.006)	.012 (.007)*	.009 (.007)	.007 (.006)	.01 (.007)	.017 (.007)***	-.006 (.01)
Price	-.003 (.003)	.001 (.003)	.001 (.003)	-.003 (.003)	.005 (.003)*	.004 (.003)	-.008 (.005)
n	162	161	162	161	162	162	82
R^2	.063	.082	.028	.048	.089	.067	.013

Notes: Ordered probit except for absenteeism equation (OLS analysis).

Absenteeism dependent variable = Log of $(P/(1–P))$ where P= absenteeism.

Coefficients given (standard errors in brackets).

R^2 is pseudo R^2 except for absenteeism equation (adjusted).

'Strategic' = above average no. of HRM practices used and hotel has formal strategy.

'Non-strategic' = above average no. of HRM practices used but hotel does not have formal strategy.

Omitted category = below average no. of HRM practices used.

The importance of internal fit

The aim of the analysis here is to assess whether hotels that claim to have introduced their HRM practices as a strategically integrated package of mutually supporting practices outperform hotels that have introduced their HRM practices in a more piecemeal manner.

Looking at Table 6.5, the results suggest that 'strategic HRM' hotels routinely outperform the 'low-HRM' hotels across all of the HR outcome measures with the exception of absenteeism. By contrast, the 'non-strategic HRM' hotels only outperform the 'low-HRM' hotels where organisational commitment is concerned. The results therefore support the hypothesis that HRM is more effective in enhancing HR outcomes where it is implemented as part of an over-arching package of mutually reinforcing practices.

The results concerning performance outcomes reported within Table 6.6 further demonstrate the impact of internal fit on performance. Whereas the 'strategic HRM' hotels outperform the 'low-HRM' hotels in terms of labour productivity, quality of service and financial performance, the 'non-strategic HRM' hotels outperform the 'low-HRM' hotels on only one of the performance measures asked about, namely financial performance. The results here would therefore seem to indicate the importance of introducing HRM practices as part of an institutionally supported, mutually reinforcing package.

Table 6.6 HRM, internal fit and performance outcomes in the hotel industry

	Labour productivity	*Quality of service*	*Financial performance*
'Strategic HRM'	.622 (.204)***	.725 (.208)***	.772 (.204)***
'Non-strategic HRM'	.212 (.274)	.33 (.271)	.564 (.27)**
Union presence	−.161 (.265)	−.204 (.268)	−.261 (.259)
50–99 employees	−.927 (.363)**	−.478 (.348)	.09 (.334)
100–199 employees	−1.318 (.373)***	−.099 (.352)	−.265 (.34)
200+ employees	−.822 (.446)*	.214 (.437)	.628 (.427)
Foreign owned	.447 (.272)	.172 (.277)	.292 (.272)
Age	.013 (.007)**	.002 (.006)	.002 (.006
Price	.002 (.003)	.008 (.003)**	.006 (.003)**
n	158	157	157
Pseudo R^2	.085	.1	.093

Notes: Ordered probit analysis. Coefficients given (standard errors in brackets).
*** significant at 1 per cent, ** significant at 5 per cent.
'Strategic' = above average no. of HR practices used and establishment has formal strategy.
'Non-strategic' = above average no. of HR practices used but establishment does not have formal strategy.
Omitted category = below average no. of HR practices used.

Conclusions

The analysis undertaken here has achieved several key findings, the first of which relates to the importance of external fit. A relationship between HRM and performance only exists amongst hotels emphasising the importance of quality enhancement and amongst hotels in the 'other' category. HRM proves ineffective where cost control is seen as the key to business strategy. This analysis therefore provides support for the contingency hypothesis that the effectiveness of HRM relies upon fit with business strategy.

To date, studies of HRM and performance have been unable to identify support for external fit (see for example Huselid, 1995; Huselid and Becker, 1996). One possible reason why the results achieved here might differ from those achieved within earlier studies is that this is a single-industry study. There is the possibility that contingency effects will be lost in multi-industry studies, as such effects may only operate in certain circumstances, while in other instances, HRM might have universal effects at the level of what Becker and Gerhart (1996: 786) describe as 'architecture'. Alternatively, business strategy may not have been measured adequately within earlier studies (Huselid (1995: 668) admits that his measures of fit are preliminary, for example). Whatever the reasons, this study is unique in that it demonstrates strong contingency effects.

The second key finding suggests HRM to be universally relevant within the hotel industry, the analysis suggesting that among the hotels with an identifiable strategy, those adopting an ethos of service quality coupled with a high number of HRM practices are performing best. It would therefore seem that a 'high-HRM quality enhancer' strategy would be the key to competitive success within hotels of the nature under investigation here, with there being little scope for a strategy based on cost reduction or price competition to achieve comparable results.

Thirdly, looking at internal fit, there is evidence that further performance gains are to be found where HRM is introduced as a mutually cohesive and institutionally supported package. Gains are less where HRM practices have been implemented in a seemingly piecemeal, uncoordinated fashion. The results here add to the conclusions reached by Guest and Hoque (1994b), Ichniowski, Shaw and Prennushi (1994) and MacDuffie (1995), who demonstrate varying degrees of support for the importance of this type of fit within their analyses.

Concerning the hotels in the 'other' category, the results suggest that HRM has a similar impact within these hotels as it does within hotels emphasising quality enhancement. As discussed earlier, while the business strategies within these hotels seem somewhat ambiguous, competing on price and quality simultaneously need not necessarily be contradictory, as a primary focus can be maintained on one of the two dimensions. One interpretation might be that, given the similarity in their behaviour to the quality enhancers, the hotels in the 'other' category are focusing primarily on quality enhancement. If this assumption is correct, adding the 'other' hotels to those in the quality enhancer category suggests that approximately 77 per cent of the hotels within the sample as a whole have identified service quality enhancement to be of central strategic importance. This would seemingly support the arguments presented by Callan (1994), Kokko and Moilanen (1997), Mattsson (1994), Olsen (1989) and Pye (1994), concerning the increasing importance of service quality within the hotel industry.

Inevitably, this analysis is subject to the caveats common to cross-sectional analyses of this nature, not least that the results here cannot be viewed as causal. All that is demonstrated is that performance is higher in situations where the hotel emphasises quality enhancement and has adopted a wide range of HRM practices. It is not known whether those practices, or indeed the quality enhancer approach to business strategy itself, have caused high performance, or whether high-performing hotels have taken the opportunity to innovate in terms of HRM. It is impossible to determine whether this is the case, especially given the limited range of controls available here for other factors that might impact on performance. To ascertain causality, longitudinal data is ideally required.

The potential for common-method variance must also be taken into consideration, given that the same respondent provided data for both the dependent and the independent variables. Common-method variance, at least in the context of the HRM and performance debate, is associated with the phenomenon of universally higher performance ratings being reported by respondents who claim to have adopted a wide range of HRM practices. However, there is no relationship between HRM and performance where the cost reducer hotels are concerned. This could be interpreted as indicative that the positive relationship between HRM and performance amongst the quality enhancer and the 'other' hotels may be more the result of genuine performance effects rather than common-method variance.

Finally, it is worth reiterating that the analysis here deliberately focuses on larger hotels, as it is amongst these hotels that an interest in HRM would be expected. As such, the results should not be viewed as representative of the hotel industry as a whole, and it may be the case that within smaller hotels, HRM has little or no role to play. The results nevertheless suggest that in larger establishments within the hotel industry, high performance is related to the adoption of a coherent package of HRM practices, coupled to a business strategy that focuses primarily on the enhancement of service quality.

Notes

1   The results reported within this chapter are also reported within the *British Journal of Industrial Relations*, 1999, 37(3).

2   Cost reducer hotels are dropped from this section, as there is little evidence of an HRM–performance relationship within these establishments in the first instance.

7 Conclusion

As argued within the opening chapter, HRM has increasingly come to be viewed as the dominant paradigm within which emergent developments in the world of work are interpreted. From a theoretical perspective, however, HRM has its roots firmly entrenched within manufacturing, where less than one in five of the UK's working population is now employed. As such, it has become increasingly important to demonstrate the validity of HRM in the services. After all, what future is there for HRM as a 'dominant paradigm' if it is deemed inapplicable to the services, within which over 76 per cent of the working population are currently employed? This book has tested this issue by presenting an analysis of the validity of HRM within the context of the UK hotel industry.

The test of the validity of HRM in the hotel industry comprised three main parts. The first concerned the extent to which techniques associated with an HRM approach have been adopted within the industry. The second concerned the extent to which the factors influencing managerial decision-making in relation to HRM in the industry correspond with the factors viewed as important within the mainstream HRM literature. The third concerned the relationship between HRM and performance. In the event, the study yielded several key findings.

How extensively has HRM been adopted in the hotel industry?

Concerning the extent to which HRM techniques have been adopted within the hotel industry, the debate has typically been characterised by a paradox. From a theoretical perspective, Lewis (1987), Nightingale (1985), Haywood (1983), Mattsson (1994) and Nailon (1989) have all argued for some time that as service quality becomes increasingly critical to competitive success, so does the need to provide staff with the skills and the motivation to be able to deliver an empowered, high quality, professional service. However, much of the empirical literature suggests a lack of interest in HRM in the industry and a greater emphasis on tight control over costs (see for example Guerrier and Lockwood, 1989a; Hales, 1987; Lockwood and Guerrier, 1989; Lucas, 1995, 1996; Price, 1994).

Only recently have empirical investigations begun to demonstrate a higher degree of the usage of techniques associated with HRM within the hotel industry (see for example Anastassova and Purcell, 1995; Buick and Muthu, 1997; Harrington and Akehurst, 1996 and Watson and D'Annunzio-Green, 1996). Supporting the conclusions reached in these studies, the results within Chapter 3 demonstrate a high reported usage of HRM practices, particularly in relation to recruitment and selection techniques, training, job design and communication and consultation. The follow-up interviews in Chapter 5 suggest that there is genuine substance behind the reported usage of HRM.

The results here, therefore, suggest that theory and practice may not be as divergent as previously believed. The techniques widely talked up within the mainstream HRM literature as 'best practice', for example, the use of sophisticated selection tests for all grades of staff, the use of regular performance appraisals, the development of career paths, the empowerment of lower levels of staff and the introduction of functional flexibility, are now being utilised within the hotel industry, at least within larger establishments, on a previously unacknowledged scale. In addition, the results suggest that HR issues are accorded a high degree of importance within the industry, not least reflected by the high proportion of hotels reporting the existence of mission statements with an explicit reference to HR issues. Indeed, mission statements with a specific reference to human resources are found in over 61 per cent of the establishments within the hotel industry sample, compared with only 38 per cent of the establishments within the manufacturing sample. Moreover, HRM is more likely to be viewed as a senior unit level management strategic concern within the hotel industry, with 76 per cent of hotel industry establishments having a formal HR strategy actively supported and formally endorsed by senior management at the site, in comparison with only 52 per cent of manufacturing industry establishments. When set in context with the conclusions reached by Guerrier and Lockwood (1989a), Hales (1987), Lockwood and Guerrier (1989), Lucas (1995, 1996) and Price (1994), these findings reflect the debate that has emerged in recent times concerning the extent to which more sophisticated approaches to HRM have been adopted within the industry.

Why might the conclusions drawn from Chapter 3 be so different from those achieved within many of the earlier analyses? Firstly, it could be due to the fact that the analysis here focuses on larger hotels. Rather than looking at a random sample of establishments across the industry as a whole, the 1995 Survey of Human Resource Management in the Hotel Industry focuses on hotels with at least 65 rooms. As is well documented, the industry is dominated by small businesses. Assuming that HRM will be considered an irrelevance within very small establishments, a random sample of hotels may well yield a lower level of adoption of techniques associated with an HRM approach than would a random sample of manufacturing establishments, within which the average establishment size will be considerably higher. However, there is no point in looking for HRM where it is unlikely to be of relevance, or unlikely to contribute to effectiveness. It may therefore be the case that across the industry as a whole, interest in HRM is lower than elsewhere. However, in hotels of the size within which HRM would be expected to have a role, usage is just as high, if not higher than within manufacturing sectors.

The difference between the conclusions reached within this analysis and those reached within earlier analyses could also result from methodology. The analysis presented here is comparative in nature. Pretty well all the previous analyses of HRM in the hotel industry have examined the industry in isolation, and have inferred from the results achieved that the industry is backward and unstrategic, in terms of the extent to which HRM has been adopted. However, there seems to be an implicit assumption within much of what is written on the hotel industry that sophisticated approaches are the norm within industries elsewhere – an assumption that is very much subject to debate. When directly comparing the usage of HRM in the hotel industry with manufacturing, there is nothing to suggest the hotel industry to be more backward or undeveloped in terms of the level of sophistication of the HRM techniques that have been adopted.

Thirdly, the results achieved within Chapter 3 could be explained by the fact that respondents to the questionnaire have misinterpreted the nature of the HRM practices asked about, are failing to apply the techniques in the spirit intended, or have simply applied the discourse or rhetoric of HRM to existing practice. However, the follow-up interviews reported within Chapter 5 suggest that there is considerable substance behind the discourse of HRM within the industry. In the hotels visited, the HRM techniques the hotels claimed to operate within their survey responses were found, for the most part, to be in place, and to be operating in the expected manner. The only exception to the rule related to single status, which most of the hotels claimed to practice, but in the event did not. Nevertheless, the HRM practices in operation in the hotels within the follow-up interview programmes were well developed, with five of the six hotels visited having achieved Investors in People accreditation. The follow-up interviews therefore provided further support for the conclusion reached within Chapter three concerning the extent to which there has been experimentation with sophisticated approaches to HRM.

The conclusions reached within this analysis suggest, therefore, that there has been genuine change within the hotel industry in recent years. Many of the analyses suggesting HRM in the hotel industry to be backward or unstrategic date back to the 1980s, whereas some of the more recent accounts are more positive in their conclusions. The evidence that HRM in the hotel industry is nowadays more sophisticated than before is therefore beginning to mount, suggesting that earlier analyses demonstrating the industry to be backward should now be viewed as somewhat dated, at least where larger hotels are concerned. Therefore, the first test of the applicability of HRM within the hotel industry, concerning the extent to which techniques associated with an HRM approach have been adopted has yielded positive results.

Influences on HRM – is the hotel industry really 'different'?

The second test of the applicability of HRM in the hotel industry concerned the factors that might influence the approach taken to HRM. Debates surround a range of potential influences on management decision-making within the mainstream HRM theory. These include the impact of product markets, the ability of management to implement change, workforce resistance to change, establishment size, the nature of trade unionism and foreign ownership. It is commonly argued, however, that managers within the hotel industry are subjected to a further set of influences, rendering the industry 'different' in many respects. Because of these differences, it has often been argued that management principles developed outside of the hotel industry are inapplicable or inappropriate.

However, as demonstrated within Chapter 2, there is considerable common ground between the influences on management decision-making seen as important within the hotel industry literature and the influences seen as important within the mainstream HRM literature. For example, both sets of literature attach an extremely high level of importance to the impact of product markets, workforce resistance to change, management ability to handle change effectively, national ownership and the nature and influence of the personnel department. The only potential influences on HRM discussed exclusively within the hotel industry literature concern workforce instability (in particular labour turnover) and the instability and seasonality of demand to be found within the hotel industry.

Moreover, not only are very few of the potential influences on management decision-making discussed within the hotel industry literature genuinely unique to the industry, but those influences, as demonstrated within the empirical analysis within Chapter 4, do not seem to have much of an impact in relation to HRM decision-making. Looking at instability of demand, Haywood (1983), Walsh (1991) and Guerrier and Lockwood (1989c) argue that both daily and seasonal demand fluctuations result in the need for large numbers of casual and part-time workers. It is true that hotels will always need part-time workers to handle daily peaks, for example to work on breakfast shifts. However, seasonal and weekly fluctuations are less of an issue within the hotels of the type being looked at within this analysis. This is for two reasons. Firstly, multi-skilling, which was emphasised in several of the hotels visited within the follow-up interview programme, enables staff to move around the hotel as the workload requires. This eases the pressure created by fluctuating headcount requirements in different parts of the hotel. Secondly, seasonal fluctuations do not seem to be an issue for many of the hotels within the sample. Only 7.64 per cent described their demand as seasonal and unpredictable. Half of the hotels stated that the demand for their services did not vary throughout the year. The seasonality that might prove influential where a small seaside holiday hotel is concerned is of little significance within the type of hotel under investigation within this sample.

In addition, daily fluctuations in demand do not seem to have much of an impact on the approach taken to HRM. There was no support within Chapter 3 for the hypothesis that there will be a negative correlation between the proportion of part-time labour used and the likelihood of HRM being practised. Part-time workers may therefore not necessarily be viewed as peripheral within the industry. If this is the case, the careful recruitment, appraising, training and the provision of career opportunities will be just as important for part-time staff as for full-time staff. Alternatively, it may be the case that HRM is applied to core workers irrespective of the proportion of part-time workers employed. Either way, instability of demand does not seem to have a major impact on the approach to HRM adopted within hotels of this nature.

It would also seem to be the case that labour turnover, the other factor seen within the literature as rendering the hotel industry 'unique', has little impact on the approach taken to HRM. Nevertheless, this does not mean that turnover can be discounted in terms of HRM policy. Nailon (1989) argues that the introduction of policies relying on shared values will be problematic where employment stability – necessary if shared values are to develop – is lacking. While this is a valid point, it is too simplistic to suggest that where turnover is high, the adoption of HRM will be low. For example, the impact of labour turnover on HRM will vary depending upon the areas of the hotel that are experiencing high levels of turnover. One respondent within the follow-up interview programme argued that high turnover would be a problem if it took place amongst front line staff, as this would impact on the introduction of the 'empowerment' programme. However, as most of the hotel's turnover took place in housekeeping and in the kitchen areas, it was not seen as problematic. Labour turnover may therefore be viewed as less of a concern if it takes place within positions to which initiatives such as 'empowerment' do not apply.

Furthermore, the follow-up interviews suggest that turnover is not viewed as an endemic, institutionalised 'fact of life', that better management will do little to cure – a point often made to argue that the hotel industry is 'different'. There is a general belief that it is possible to reduce labour turnover via the introduction of HRM techniques, but that turnover will always be higher than elsewhere because of the high proportion of foreign and young workers within the industry.

The influences seen as unique to the hotel industry therefore have little impact on management decision-making in relation to HRM. By contrast, the major influences on HRM seem to be those discussed within both the hotel industry literature and within the mainstream literature. As such, there is no evidence to support the hypothesis that hotels are in any way 'unique', and it would appear that the key influences on management decision-making in relation to HRM in the hotel industry are just the same as the influences on management decision-making elsewhere.

One of the most important of these influences appears to be the nature of the product market, on which there is a degree of disagreement within the industry. Haywood (1983), Nightingale (1985) and Lewis (1987) argue that effectiveness within hotels increasingly rests on the satisfaction of evolving customer expectations. Conversely, Shamir (1978) and Larmour (1983) argue that the market dictates a need for a tight control over costs and price competition. Robinson and Wallace (1984) suggest that this position is reflected by the high usage of temporary workers across the industry as a whole. The results achieved within this analysis support the former of these propositions. Just under half of the sample expressly state that the key to their competitive strategy is the provision of a high quality service, compared with only 23 per cent who emphasise the importance of cost control or price factors. Of the remaining hotels, both within the qualitative and the quantitative analyses, the hotels classified as 'other' would seem to be more akin to the quality enhancers than the cost reducers. If this is the case, and these hotels are added to those explicitly specifying the importance of quality enhancement, the implication is that approximately 77 per cent of the hotels within the sample have identified the need for service quality as the key to competitive advantage.

What of the impact of business strategy on the approach taken to HRM? Schuler and Jackson (1987) within the HRM literature, and also Jones (1983), Lefever and Reich (1991) and Wycott (1984) within the hotel industry literature, argue that where an establishment emphasises the importance of service quality within its business strategy, it is also likely to view an HRM approach aimed at the generation of staff commitment to service quality goals as important. This argument is supported by the analysis in Chapter 4. Hotels specifying quality enhancement to be the key to competitive strategy are indeed more likely to have adopted HRM than are hotels emphasising cost reduction. The results therefore demonstrate that the nature of the product market, which is seen as highly influential in determining the approach taken to HRM within the mainstream literature, is also highly influential within the hotel industry.

Also important is national ownership. Lucas and Laycock (1991) and Price (1994) find foreign-owned hotels to have adopted more sophisticated approaches to HRM. The results within Chapter 4 corroborate this argument.

Other factors discussed as potentially important within both the hotel industry literature and in the mainstream HRM literature have a somewhat more ambiguous impact. Firstly, looking at managerial capacity for strategic decision-making, and in particular, the strategic impact of personnel departments, the results in Chapters 3 and 4 suggest that personnel departments are no more poorly resourced than personnel departments in other sectors of the economy. Personnel specialists are just as likely to be in evidence, they are just as well qualified, and are just as likely to have access to support staff as are personnel specialists in other industries.

These findings support conclusions reached by Lucas (1995, 1996) and Price (1994). However, there is little evidence within Chapter 4 to suggest that unit-level personnel are responsible for the introduction of a more sophisticated approach to HRM. This is consistent with the finding that hotels that are part of a chain are more likely to have adopted HRM. It seems that HRM policy initiatives have been introduced top-down in many instances.

This is not to suggest that unit-level personnel departments completely lack any strategic input. The follow-up interviews suggest that unit-level personnel departments are responsible for tailoring top-down policy initiatives to the local situation. Also, dissemination of 'best practice' developed at unit-level is facilitated by regular meetings between unit-level personnel managers. However, it would also seem that unit level personnel departments are responsible for the day-to-day recruitment and selection needs generated by high levels of labour turnover. Where labour turnover is high, it is more likely that the hotel will have a personnel specialist.

Workforce resistance to change, another potential influence on the approach taken to HRM discussed within both the HRM and the hotel literature, also seems to have little impact. The results within Chapter 4 demonstrate workforce resistance to technical change to be minimal. Many of the technical changes introduced within the hotels in the follow-up surveys concerned computerisation. Staff have tended to be positive about such changes, appreciating the opportunity to learn new skills. Support amongst the workforce for the introduction of functional flexibility, as noted by Guerrier and Lockwood (1989c), was also identified within the follow-up interviews conducted here. Several interviewees suggested that operatives appreciate the chance to broaden their range of skills and to be able to perform a wider range of functions within their everyday job roles. Organisational change, frequently involving delayering and an increase in responsibility for management, met with higher resistance than technical change, in particular from the managers whose job roles were affected significantly.

Turning to establishment size, it is commonly argued that the hotel industry is dominated by small establishments within which HRM is irrelevant, with informal face-to-face interpersonal communication taking the place of formal practices (Price, 1994). It may well be the case that within such small hotels, HRM is irrelevant. This analysis, however, says nothing on these establishments, as the 1995 Survey of Human Resource Management in the Hotel Industry only looks at hotels with more than 25 employees. However, the results do suggest that in hotels with 25 or more employees, there is no linear correlation between hotel size and the likelihood of HRM having been adopted. It is not the case therefore that HRM is only practised in the largest hotels within the sample. Given that the smallest size dummy used within the analysis was for establishments with between 25 and 49 employees, it would seem that if there is a minimum size threshold below which HRM becomes irrelevant, that size threshold is quite low.

Looking at unionisation, the results here suggest that the weak unionisation in existence within the industry has little or no impact on management prerogative, though whether managers choose to use that prerogative to introduce HRM or to unilaterally impose practices aimed at labour intensification or cost cutting, is a different matter. Within the follow-up interview programme, the interviewees within the 'HRM' hotels stressed the importance of non-unionism in terms of being free to experiment and innovate. Within the 'non-HRM cost reducer', however, the lack of a union had enabled the unilateral introduction of cost-cutting measures during the recession of the early 1990s.

Finally, there is no evidence to suggest that where hotels are part of a diversified conglomerate business, they are less likely to have adopted HRM than are hotels that are part of single, related or dominant businesses. There is therefore no support for the hypothesis presented by Purcell (1989) and Kirkpatrick, Davies and Oliver (1992).

Overall, this analysis suggests that the strongest influences on HRM decision-making in the hotel industry relate to product markets and to ownership. These influences are recognised as important within the mainstream HRM literature also. By contrast, the influences that are often seen as making the hotel industry 'unique' – daily and seasonal demand fluctuations and high labour turnover – have no impact. There is no evidence therefore that the influences on management decision-making in the hotel industry are any different from the influences on management decision-making elsewhere. As such, there are no grounds to argue that the industry is in any way 'different', or that theory developed within the mainstream management literature should be viewed as inapplicable.

HRM and performance

The final test of the relevance of HRM within the hotel industry concerned the relationship between HRM and performance. The results in Chapter 6 suggest that the better performing hotels are indeed those that have adopted a quality enhancer approach to business strategy, coupled with HRM. Those that have introduced their HRM practices in a strategic manner as part of a package of practices consciously integrated and supportive of each other, are performing even better. Looking at hotels emphasising cost reduction, there is no relationship between the adoption of HRM and performance whatsoever.

While many studies have demonstrated a relationship between HRM and performance (for example, Arthur, 1994; Delaney and Huselid; 1996, Huselid,

1995), fewer have been able to establish a relationship between HRM, performance and the approach taken to business strategy, despite what Huselid (1995) describes as 'compelling arguments' that HRM should only prove effective in certain circumstances. This analysis demonstrates support for this so far elusive yet 'compelling' linkage between HRM, business strategy and performance. As such, these results represent a considerable advance on previous work examining the HRM and performance relationship.

Given that the hotels which either continue to focus on cost reduction, or fail to realise the potential of a coherent package of HRM practices would seem to lose out in terms of organisational performance, the results within Chapter 6 also have prescriptive implications. A fair proportion of the hotels within the sample seem to have already realised this. Approximately 46 per cent specify quality enhancement as being the key to competitive strategy, and of these, approximately 55 per cent have adopted an approach to HRM congruent with their business strategy. Nevertheless, the fact remains that 23 per cent of the hotels within the sample are focusing on cost reduction or price competition, and a further 21 per cent have specified quality enhancement to be the key to competitive success, yet are not pursuing an identifiable HRM approach. The prescriptive implication is that these hotels should consider a reappraisal of the priorities within both their business strategies and their HRM strategies, and consider the adoption of a business strategy that focuses on high service quality coupled with a coherent, mutually supporting package of HRM practices.

Once again, however, the embryonic nature of these results should be emphasised, not to mention the fact that they are cross-sectional and therefore not necessarily causal. There is a need for further empirical analysis testing in greater depth the relationship between HRM and performance in the hotel industry, ideally using longitudinal data. If further studies can demonstrate linkages between HRM and performance similar to those found here, considerable weight will be added to the prescriptive argument that hotels should be encouraged to a strategically integrated package of HRM practices coupled with a quality enhancer approach to business strategy.

A re-focusing of hotel industry research?

The results presented within this book would suggest that the theoretical propositions relating to HRM – as developed within the mainstream HRM literature – are applicable within the hotel industry. The hotels within the sample have adopted a wide range of HRM techniques and are subject to a similar set of influences in relation to HRM decision-making as are establishments elsewhere.

HRM would also seem to contribute to performance within the industry. This is good news for researchers whose primary interest lies within the hotel industry itself, as it would seem that the HRM theory discussed in Chapter 1 provides a sound theoretical framework within which future hotel industry empirical analysis can be located. In addition, it is good news for HRM as a theory, in that the analysis presented here demonstrates the predictions and underlying assumptions within HRM theory to be relevant within a service-related context.

The results also suggest that hotels of the nature under investigation within this analysis may no longer be deserving of their image as 'bad employers'. The analysis shows that a high proportion of hotels within the UK, many of which have Investors in People accreditation and have well-developed personnel departments, are making efforts to develop their staff, training them in the skills necessary to provide a high quality professional service. Inevitably, as in all industries, there will also be examples of poor practice. Nevertheless, it is perhaps time researchers stopped highlighting examples of 'bad management', and branding the industry as under-developed or backward, and started identifying approaches to hotel management capable of generating high performance. If researchers can indeed identify examples of performance-enhancing best practice, encourage their dissemination and assist in their implementation, they will be in a position to make a far greater contribution towards the achievement of competitive success within the industry.

Bibliography

Anastassova, L. and Purcell, K. (1995) 'Human resource management in the Bulgarian hotel industry: from command to empowerment', *International Journal of Hospitality Management* 14,2: 171–85.

Armistead, C. (ed.) (1994) *The Future of Services Management*, London: Kogan Page.

Armstrong, P. (1989) 'Limits and possibilities for HRM in an age of management accountancy', in J. Storey (ed.), *New Perspectives on Human Resource Management*, London: Routledge.

Arthur, J. (1994) 'Effects of human resource systems on manufacturing performance and turnover', *Academy of Management Journal* 37,3: 670–87.

Atkinson, J. (1984) 'Manpower strategies for flexible organisations', *Personnel Management* 16,8: 28–31.

Automobile Association (1994) *The Hotel Guide 1995*, Basingstoke: AA Publishing.

Beaumont, P. (1992) 'The US human resource management literature: a review', in G. Salaman (ed.) *Human Resource Strategies*, London: Sage.

Beaumont, P. (1993) *Human Resource Management, Key Concepts and Skills*, London: Sage.

Beaumont, P., Cressey, P. and Jakobsen, P. (1990) 'Some key industrial relations features of West German subsidiaries in Britain', *Employee Relations* 12,6: 3–8.

Becker, B. and Gerhart, B., (1996) 'The impact of human resource management on organisational performance: progress and prospects', *Academy of Management Journal* 39,4: 779–801.

Beer, M., Spector, B., Lawrence, P., Quinn Mills, D. and Walton, R. (1984) *Managing Human Assets*, New York: Free Press.

Beer, M., Spector, B., Lawrence, P., Quinn Mills, D. and Walton, R. (1985) *Human Resource Management: A General Manager's Perspective*, Glencoe, IL: Free Press.

Blyton, P. and Turnbull, P. (1992) 'Human resource management: debates, dilemmas and contradictions', in P. Blyton and P. Turnbull (eds) *Reassessing Human Resource Management*, London: Sage.

Blyton, P. and Turnbull, P. (eds) (1992) *Reassessing Human Resource Management*, London: Sage.

Boella, M. (1986) 'A review of personnel management in the private sector of the British hospitality industry', *International Journal of Hospitality Management* 5,1: 29–36.

Boxall, P. and Dowling, P. (1990) 'Human resource management and the industrial relations tradition', *Labour and Industry* 3: 195–214.

Buick, I. and Muthu, G. (1997) 'An investigation of the current practices of in-house employee training and development within hotels in Scotland', *Service Industries Journal* 17,4: 652–68.

Callan, R.J. (1994) 'Quality assurance certification for hospitality marketing, sales and customer services', *Service Industries Journal* 14,4: 482–98.

Capelli, P. and McKersie, R. (1987) 'Management strategy and the redesign of work rules', *Journal of Management Studies* 24,5: 441–62.

Commission on Industrial Relations (1971) *The Hotel and Catering Industry Part I: Hotels and Restaurants*, London: HMSO.

Daly, A., Hitchens, D. and Wagner, K. (1985) 'Productivity, machinery and skills in a sample of British and German manufacturing plants', *National Institute Economic Review* February: 48–61.

Daniel, W.W. (1987) *Workplace Industrial Relations and Technical Change*, London: Frances Pinter.

Delaney, J. and Huselid, M. (1996) 'The impact of human resource management on perceptions of organisational performance', *Academy of Management Journal* 39,4: 949–69.

Denvir, A. and McMahon, F. (1992) 'Labour turnover in London hotels and the cost effectiveness of preventative measures', *International Journal of Hospitality Management* 11,2: 143–54.

Department of National Heritage (1996) 'People working in tourism and hospitality', *Tourism: Competing With the Best*, Part 3.

Drenth, P., Koopman, P. and Wilpert, B. (eds) (1996) *Organisational Decision-Making Under Different Economic and Political Conditions*, Amsterdam: Royal Dutch Academy.

Evans, P. and Lorange, P. (1989) 'Two logics behind human resource management', in P. Evans, Y. Doz and A. Laurent (eds) *Human Resource Management in International Firms*, Basingstoke: Macmillan.

Fernie, S. and Metcalf, D. (1995) 'Participation, contingent pay, representation and workplace performance', *British Journal of Industrial Relations* 33,3: 379–415.

Finegold, D. and Soskice, D. (1988) 'The failure of training in Britain: analysis and prescription', *Oxford Review of Economic Policy* 4,3: 21–53.

Gabriel, Y. (1988) *Working Lives in Catering*, London: Routledge and Kegan Paul.

Gilbert, D. and Guerrier, Y. (1997) 'UK hospitality managers past and present', *Service Industries Journal* 17,1: 115–32.

Guerrier, Y. and Lockwood, A. (1989a) 'Developing hotel managers: a reappraisal', *International Journal of Hospitality Management* 8,2: 82–8.

Guerrier, Y. and Lockwood, A. (1989b) 'Core and peripheral employees in hotel operations', *Personnel Review* 18,1: 9–15.

Guerrier, Y. and Lockwood, A. (1989c) 'Managing flexible working in hotels', *Service Industries Journal*, 9,3: 406–19.

Guest, D. (1987) 'Human resource management and industrial relations', *Journal of Management Studies* 24,5: 503–21.

Guest, D. (1989) 'HRM: its implications for industrial relations and trade unions', in J. Storey (ed.) *New Perspectives on Human Resource Management*, London: Routledge.

Guest, D. (1995) 'Human resource management, trade unions and industrial relations', in J. Storey (ed.) *Human Resource Management: A Critical Text*, London: Routledge.

Guest, D. (1996) 'The influence of national ownership on the nature and effectiveness of human resource management in UK greenfield establishments: the peculiar case of Germany', in P. Drenth, P. Koopman and B. Wilpert (eds) *Organisational Decision Making Under Different Economic and Political Conditions*, Amsterdam: Royal Dutch Academy.

Guest, D. (1997) 'Human resource management: a review and research agenda', *International Journal of Human Resource Management* 8,3: 263–76.

Guest, D. and Dewe, P. (1991) 'Company or trade union: which wins workers' allegiance?', *British Journal of Industrial Relations* 29,1: 75–96.

Guest, D. and Hoque, K. (1993) *Are Greenfield Sites Better at HRM?*, CEP Working Paper No 435, London: LSE.

Guest, D. and Hoque, K. (1994a) 'An assessment and further analysis of the 1990 Workplace Industrial Relations Survey' in D. Guest, S. Tyson, N. Doherty, K. Hoque and C. Viney. *The Contribution of Personnel Management to Organisational Performance: moving the debate on*, Issues in Personnel Management No. 9, London: IPD.

Guest, D. and Hoque, K. (1994b) 'The good, the bad and the ugly: employee relations in new non-union workplaces', *Human Resource Management Journal* 5,1: 1–14.

Guest, D. and Hoque, K. (1994c) *Human Resource Management in Greenfield Sites: Preliminary Survey Results*, CEP Working Paper No. 530, London: LSE.

Guest, D. and Hoque, K. (1996) 'Human resource management and the new industrial relations', in I. Beardwell (ed.) *Contemporary Industrial Relations*, Oxford: OUP.

Guest, D. and Hoque, K. (1996) 'National ownership and HR practices in UK greenfield sites', *Human Resource Management Journal* 6,4: 50–74.

Hales, C. (1987) 'Quality of working life, jobs redesign and participation in a service industry: a rose by any other name?', *Service Industries Journal* 7,2: 253–73.

Handy, C. (1985) *Understanding Organisations*, Harmondsworth: Penguin.

Harrington, D. and Akehurst, G. (1996) 'Service quality and business performance in the UK hotel industry', *International Journal of Hospitality Management* 15,3: 283–98.

Haywood, K. (1983) 'Assessing the quality of hospitality services', *International Journal of Hospitality Management* 2,4: 165–77.

Hendry, C. and Pettigrew, A. (1986) 'The practice of strategic human resource management', *Personnel Review* 15,5: 3–8.

158 *Human resource management in the hotel industry*

Hendry, C. and Pettigrew, A. (1990) 'Human resource management: an agenda for the 1990s', *International Journal of Human Resource Management* 1,1: 17–44.

Huselid, M. (1995) 'The impact of human resource management on turnover, productivity and corporate financial performance', *Academy of Management Journal* 38: 635–72.

Huselid, M. and Becker, B. (1996) 'Methodological issues in cross-sectional and panel estimates of the human resource–firm performance link', *Industrial Relations* 35,3: 400–22.

Hyman, R. (1991) 'Plus ca change? The theory of production and the production of theory', in A. Pollert (ed.) *Farewell to Flexibility?*, Oxford: Blackwell.

Ichniowski, C., Shaw, K. and Prennushi, G. (1994) *The effects of human resource management practices on productivity*, Columbia University.

Iverson, R. and Deery, M. (1997) 'Turnover culture in the hospitality industry', *Human Resource Management Journal* 7,4: 71–82.

Johns, N. (1992) 'Quality management in the hospitality industry: part 2. Applications, systems and techniques', *International Journal of Contemporary Hospitality Management* 4,4: 3–7.

Johnson, K. (1985) 'Labour turnover in hotels – revisited', *Service Industries Journal* 5,2: 135–52.

Jones, P. (1983) 'The restaurant – a place for quality control and product maintenance?', *International Journal of Hospitality Management* 2,2: 93–100.

Jones, P. and Davies, A. (1991) 'Empowerment: a study of general managers in four-star hotel properties in the UK', *International Journal of Hospitality Management* 10,3: 211–17.

Kane, J. (1986) 'Participative management as a key to hospitality excellence', *International Journal of Hospitality Management* 5,3: 149–51.

Keenoy, T. (1990) 'HRM: a case of the wolf in sheep's clothing', *Personnel Review* 19,2: 3–9.

Keep, E. (1989) 'A training scandal?', in K. Sisson (ed.) *Personnel Management in Britain*, Oxford: Blackwell.

Kelliher, C. and Johnson, K. (1987) 'Personnel management in hotels – some empirical observations', *International Journal of Hospitality Management*, 6,2: 103–8.

Kelliher, C. and Johnson, K. (1997) 'Personnel management in hotels – an update', *Progress in Tourism and Hospitality Research* 3,4: 321–31.

King, C. (1984) 'Service-oriented quality control', *Cornell Hotel and Restaurant Administration Quarterly* February: 92.

Kirkpatrick, I., Davies, A. and Oliver, N. (1992) 'Decentralisation: friend or foe of human resource management?' in P. Blyton and P. Turnbull (eds) *Reassessing Human Resource Management*, London: Sage.

Knights, D. and Wilmott, H. (eds) (1989) *Labour Process Theory*, London: Macmillan.

Knox, S. and Thompson, K. (1994) 'Grocery retailing in the single European market – developments in structure, strategy and share', in C. Armistead (ed.) *The Future of Services Management*, London: Kogan Page.

Kochan, T. and Barocci, T. (1985) *Human Resource Management and Industrial Relations: Text, Readings and Cases*, Boston: Little Brown.

Kochan, T. and Dyer, L. (1992) *Managing transformational change: the role of human resource professionals*, Working Paper, Alfred P. Sloan School of Management, Cambridge, MA: MIT.

Kokko, T. and Moilanen, T. (1997) 'Personalisation of services as a tool for more developed buyer–seller interactions', *International Journal of Hospitality Management* 16,3: 297–304.

Larmour, R. (1983) 'Some problems faced by managers in the hotel and catering industry', *International Journal of Hospitality Management* 2,2: 89–92.

Lashley, C. (1995) 'Towards an understanding of employee empowerment in hospitality services', *International Journal of Contemporary Hospitality Management* 7,1: 27–32.

Lashley, C. (1996) 'Research issues for employee empowerment in hospitality organisations', *International Journal of Hospitality Management* 15,4: 333–46.

Lefever, M. and Reich, A. (1991) 'Shared values: no longer dirty words in company success', *International Journal of Hospitality Management* 10,4: 307–12.

Legge, K. (1995) *Human Resource Management: Rhetorics and Realities*, London: Macmillan.

Lewis, R. (1987)'The measurement of gaps in the quality of hotel services', *International Journal of Hospitality Management* 6,2: 83–8.

Littler, C. (1989) 'The labour process debate: a theoretical review 1974–84', in D. Knights and H. Wilmott (eds), *Labour Process Theory*, London: Macmillan.

Lockwood, A. and Guerrier, Y. (1989) 'Flexible working practices in the hospitality industry: current strategies and future potential', *Journal of Contemporary Hospitality Management* 1,1: 11–16.

Lucas, R. (1993) 'Hospitality industry employment: emerging trends', *International Journal of Contemporary Hospitality Management* 5,5: 23–6.

Lucas, R. (1995) *Managing Employee Relations in the Hotel and Catering Industry*, London: Cassell.

Lucas, R. (1996) 'Industrial relations in hotels and catering: neglect and paradox?', *British Journal of Industrial Relations* 34,2: 267–86.

Lucas, R. and Laycock, J. (1991) 'An interactive personnel function for managing budget hotels', *International Journal of Contemporary Hospitality Management* 3,3: 33–36.

Lucas, R. and Wood, R. (1993) 'Introduction', *Employee Relations* 15,2: 4–7.

Mabey, C. and Salaman, G. (1995) *Strategic Human Resource Management*, Oxford: Blackwell.

Macauley, I. and Wood, R. (1992) *Hard Cheese: A Study of Hotel and Catering Employment in Scotland*, Scottish Low Pay Unit.

MacDuffie, J. (1995) 'Human resource bundles and manufacturing performance: organisational logic and flexible production systems in the world auto industry', *Industrial and Labour Relations Review* 48,2: 197–221.

Macfarlane, A. (1982) 'Trade unionism and the employer in hotels and restaurants', *International Journal of Hospitality Management* 1,1: 35–43.

Marginson, P., Armstrong, P., Edwards, P. and Purcell, J. with Hubbard, N. (1993) 'The control of industrial relations in large companies: an initial analysis of the second company level industrial relations survey', *Warwick Papers in Industrial Relations* 45, Warwick: Industrial Relations Research Unit.

Mars, G. and Mitchell, P. (1976) *Room for Reform*, Milton Keynes: Open University Press.

Mars, G., Bryant, D. and Mitchell, P. (1979) *Manpower Problems in the Hotel and Catering Industry*, Farnborough: Gower.

Mathe, H. and Perras, C. (1994) 'The challenges of globalisation in the service industry', in C. Armistead (ed.) *The Future of Services Management*, London: Kogan Page.

Mattsson, J. (1994) 'Improving service quality in person to person encounters: integrating findings from a multidisciplinary review', *Service Industries Journal* 14,1: 45–61.

Miles, R. and Snow, C. (1984) 'Designing strategic human resource systems', *Organisational Dynamics* Summer: 36–52.

Miller, D. (1986) 'Configurations of strategy and structures: towards a synthesis', *Strategic Management Journal* 7: 233–49.

Mills, R. (1986) 'Managing the service encounter', *Cornell Hotel and Restaurant Administration Quarterly* February, 39–43.

Millward, N., Stevens, M., Smart, D. and Hawes, W. (1992) *Workplace Industrial Relations in Transition*, Aldershot: Dartmouth.

Mintzberg, H. (1987) 'Crafting strategy', *Harvard Business Review* 65,4: 65–75.

Mullins, L. (1993) 'The hotel and the open systems model of organisational analysis', *Service Industries Journal* 13,1: 1–16.

Nailon, P. (1989) 'Editorial', *International Journal of Hospitality Management* 8,2: 77–8.

Nightingale, M. (1985) 'The hospitality industry: defining quality for a quality assurance programme – a study of perceptions', *Service Industries Journal* 5,1: 9–22.

Office for National Statistics (1998) *Labour Market Trends*, November.

Office for National Statistics (1999) *Labour Market Trends*, January.

Ohlin, J. and West, J. (1994) 'An analysis of the effect of fringe benefit offerings on the turnover on hourly housekeeping workers in the hospitality industry', *International Journal of Hospitality Management* 12,4: 323–36.

Oliver, N. and Wilkinson, B. (1989) 'Japanese manufacturing techniques and personnel and industrial relations practice in Britain: evidence and implications', *British Journal of Industrial Relations* 27,1: 73–91.

Oliver, N. and Wilkinson, B. (1992) *The Japanisation of British Industry; New Developments in the 1990s* (2nd edn), Oxford: Blackwell.

Olsen, M. (1989) 'Issues facing multi-unit hospitality organisations in a maturing market', *Journal of Contemporary Hospitality Management* 1,2: 3–11.

Peters, T. and Waterman, R. (1982) *In Search of Excellence*, New York: Harper and Row.

Piore, M. and Sabel, C. (1984) *The Second Industrial Divide*, New York: Basic Books.

Pollert, A. (ed.) (1991) *Farewell to Flexibility?*, Oxford: Blackwell.

Porter, M. (1980) *Competitive Strategy: Techniques for Analysing Industries and Competitors*, New York: Free Press.

Porter, M. (1985) *Competitive Advantage: Creating and Sustaining Superior Performance*, New York: Free Press.

Prais, S.J., Jarvis, V. and Wagner, K. (1989) 'Productivity and vocational skills in services in Britain and Germany: hotels', *National Institute Economic Review* November: 52–74.

Price, L. (1994) 'Poor personnel practice in the hotel and catering industry: does it matter?', *Human Resource Management Journal* 4,4: 44–62.

Purcell, J. (1989) 'The impact of corporate strategy on human resource management', in J. Storey (ed.) *New Perspectives on Human Resource Management*, London: Routledge.

Purcell, J. (1991) 'The rediscovery of the management prerogative: the management of labour relations in the 1980s', *Oxford Review of Economic Policy* 7,1: 33–43.

Pye, G. (1994) 'Customer service: a model for empowerment', *International Journal of Hospitality Management* 13,1: 1–5.

Quinn, J. (1992) *Intelligent Enterprise: A Knowledge and Service Based Paradigm For Industry*, New York: Free Press.

Rajan, A. (1987) *Services – The Second Industrial Revolution?*, London: Institute of Manpower Studies.

Ramsay, H. (1991) 'Reinventing the wheel? A review of the development and performance of employee involvement', *Human Resource Management Journal* 1,4: 1–22.

Riley, M. (1993) 'Back to the future: lessons from the free market experience', *Employee Relations* 15,2: 8–15.

Robinson, O. and Wallace, J. (1984) 'Earnings in the hotel and catering industry in Britain', *Service Industries Journal* 4,2: 143–60.

Ross, G. (1995) 'Management–employee divergences among hospitality industry employee service quality ideals', *International Journal of Hospitality Management* 14,1: 11–24.

Salaman, G. (ed.) (1992) *Human Resource Strategies*, London: Sage.

Schaffer, J. (1984) 'Strategy, organisation structure and success in the lodging industry', *International Journal of Hospitality Management* 3,4: 159–65.

Schuler, R. (1989) 'Strategic human resource management and industrial relations', *Human Relations* 42,2: 157–84.

Schuler, R. and Jackson, S. (1987) 'Linking competitive strategies with human resource management practices', *Academy of Management Executive* 1,3: 207–19.

Segal-Horn, S. (1994) 'Are the services going global?', in C. Armistead (ed.) *The Future of Services Management*, London: Kogan Page.

Senior, M. and Morphew, R. (1990) 'Competitive strategies in the budget hotel sector', *International Journal of Contemporary Hospitality Management* 2,3: 3–9.

Shamir, B. (1978) 'Between bureaucracy and hospitality – some organisational characteristics of hotels', *Journal of Management Studies* 15,3: 285–307.

Shamir, B. (1981) 'The workplace as a community: the case of British hotels', *Industrial Relations Journal* 12,6: 45–56.

Sisson, K. (1993) 'In search of HRM', *British Journal of Industrial Relations* 31,2: 201–10.

Sisson, K. and Storey, J. (1990) 'Limits to transformation: human resource management in the British context', *Industrial Relations Journal* 21,1: 60–5.

Steedman, H. and Wagner, K. (1987) 'A second look at productivity, machinery and skills in Britain and Germany', *National Institute Economic Review*, November: 84–95.

Storey, J. (ed.) (1989) *New Perspectives on Human Resource Management*, London: Routledge.

Storey, J. (1992) *Developments in the Management of Human Resources*, Oxford: Blackwell.

Storey, J. (ed.) (1995) *Human Resource Management: A Critical Text*, London: Routledge.

Teare, R. (1996) 'Hospitality operations: patterns in management, service improvement and business performance', *International Journal of Contemporary Hospitality Management* 8,7: 63–74.

Teare, R. and Brotherton, B. (1991) 'Assessing human resource needs and priorities', *International Journal of Contemporary Hospitality Management* 2,2: 5–7.

Tichy, N., Fombrun, C. and Devanna, M. (1982) 'Strategic human resource management', *Sloan Management Review* 11,3: 47–61.

Trades Union Congress (1994) *Human Resource Management: A Trade Union Response*, London: TUC.

Trevor, M. and White, M. (1983) *Under Japanese Management*, London: Heinemann.

Walsh, T. (1991) '"Flexible" employment in the retail and hotel trades', in A. Pollert (ed.) *Farewell to Flexibility?*, Oxford: Blackwell.

Walton, R. (1985) 'From control to commitment in the workplace', *Harvard Business Review* 63, March–April: 76–84.

Watson, S. and D'Annunzio-Green, N. (1996) 'Implementing cultural change through human resources: the elusive organisational alchemy?', *International Journal of Contemporary Hospitality Management* 8,2: 25–30.

Whipp, R. (1992) 'Human resource management, competition and strategy: some productive tensions', in P. Blyton and P. Turnbull (eds) *Reassessing Human Resource Management,* London: Sage.

Whittington, R. (1993) *What is Strategy and Does it Matter?*, London: Routledge.

Whyte, W. (1948) *Human Relations in the Restaurant Industry*, New York: McGraw-Hill.

Wickens, P. (1987) *The Road to Nissan: Flexibility, Quality, Teamwork*, Basingstoke: Macmillan.

Wood, R. (1992) *Working in Hotels and Catering*, London: Routledge.

Wood, R. and Macauley, I. (1989) 'R for turnover: retention programs that work', *The Cornell Hotel Restaurant Administration Quarterly* 30,1: 79–90.

Wood, S. (1996) 'How different are human resource practices in Japanese "transplants" in the UK?', *Industrial Relations* 35,4: 511–25.

Wood, S. and Albanese, M., (1995) 'Can we speak of a high commitment management on the shop floor?', *Journal of Management Studies* 32,2: 215–47.

Wood, S. and de Menezes, L. (1998) 'High commitment management in the UK: evidence from the Workplace Industrial Relations Survey, and Employers' Manpower and Skills Practices Survey', *Human Relations* 51,4: 485–515.

Wycott, D. (1984) 'New tools for service quality', *Cornell Hotel and Restaurant Administration Quarterly* November: 78–91.

Index